THE AMAZON EXPAN

Learn how to skyrocket your sales, sell globally and make your brand an international success

UPDATED FOR 2018

KIRI MASTERS

Founder & CEO of Bobsled Marketing

CONTENTS

Printed in the United States of America. First Printing: 2016. Developed with Laura Hanly Content Marketing Agency.

Published by BobsledMarketing.com

Resources Page: http://www.bobsledmarketing.com/amazon-expansion-plan-resources

ISBN: 978-0-9981901-8-1 (Kindle Edition)
ISBN: 978-0-9981901-9-8 (Paperback Edition)

Chapter One: Getting Started

Welcome to The Amazon Expansion Plan. I'm so glad you picked up this book, and that you're ready to grow your presence on Amazon. This book is a complete playbook — no matter what stage your company is at, you'll get clear, actionable strategies that will help you expand efficiently. My team and I put these strategies to use daily at Bobsled Marketing to help over a hundred brands build strong, profitable Amazon stores.

There are three key areas we're going to explore in depth over the course of this book. In Part One, we'll delve into the nitty-gritty details of how Amazon operates, what's required of you to get involved, and how to handle the various elements at play in setting up your assortment. In Part Two, we'll cover how to optimize your product assortment with a number of proven strategies, and finally in Part Three, you'll learn how to expand your reach by establishing your brand in Amazon's international marketplaces.

One of the most important things you're going to learn from this book is about which of Amazon's sales programs is right for your brand. We'll talk about the Vendor Program, Fulfilled by Amazon, the Merchant program — there are many different ways of selling on Amazon. There are also many strategies you can use to make them work for you, which we'll cover in depth.

The next topic we will cover in a lot of detail is optimizing your Amazon channel. You want to maximize all of your listings, and you do that by developing a strong response to the three key elements of Amazon's search algorithm: relevance, conversion and sales velocity. Paid search advertising has become a critical element in building and maintaining momentum for product listings on Amazon, and so we have a new chapter dedicated to this topic for the 2018 edition of this book.

The final thing you'll learn is how to expand into Amazon's international marketplaces. You'll discover which marketplaces are available to you, how to handle the logistics of importing, what your tax requirements will be, and how to manage inventory and customer service in territories far removed from your home country.

If your brand is not yet on Amazon, and you are reading this book to familiarize yourself with the process before you take the plunge, I recommend starting just with the first couple of chapters. Once you've got a grip on the Amazon 'landscape', you can focus on getting your store set up and then come back to the chapters on optimization and international expansion when you're ready.

If you already have an Amazon presence and are specifically looking for growth, you could probably skim the first section on Amazon's systems and focus on the optimization strategies, then explore the international expansion chapters. Now, let me be clear — international expansion is a *big* undertaking. It requires a lot of careful planning and coordination, and I believe you should only attempt it once you have a reliable, replicable system under control in your home marketplace.

That said, Amazon is only going to continue to grow, both in the key US market and in new international markets. With an estimated 500 million or more products listed on Amazon at the time of writing, it's becoming quite rare for any brand with an online presence *not* to be on the platform. Some businesses are resistant to adding Amazon to their sales channels, whether it's because they have concerns about channel conflict, or they don't think they have the resources to handle it, or they simply don't want to relinquish any control of their brand. As consumer expectations evolve, however, each business has to make a very conscious decision if they are not going to list their products on Amazon (and *not* addressing the issue still effectively makes that decision). If a consumer can't find your brand on Amazon, they're going to wonder why — many people use Amazon as a search engine to do their product research, and having your products listed builds credibility and trust with customers. Being on Amazon is becoming synonymous with being a modern consumer brand.

Another big area of growth on Amazon is the B2B market. Amazon for Business was established in 2015 and generated a billion dollars in sales in its first year. When you think about the type of products required by government bodies, universities, medical institutions and large corporations, there is a purchase volume there that B2C can't compete with. All those businesses have huge demand for consumable products, and there is a big opportunity to get involved in Amazon's foray into this area. Most brands have at least a few products that would be suitable to sell B2B — whether as gifts for employees or clients, as supplies for offices or other physical locations, or as tools that amplify the buyer's ability to do business. This is the first time the business market is being served effectively by an ecommerce platform, so all brands should be considering the business market and how Amazon can be leveraged to enter this market.

There are many programs in the works at Amazon at any given time, and staying abreast of them is a full-time job in itself. For example, at the time of the 2018 edition of this book, Amazon was moving on…

- Integrating its $13.7 billion purchase of the Whole Foods grocery store chain, which will give Amazon a footprint of 450 physical stores in the United States. Amazon also accessed the burgeoning '365 by Whole Foods' brand of grocery items, which essentially sold out in the first week of launching on Amazon.com

- Launching more private label brands of their own. Through their marketplace, Amazon has access to reams of data about consumer purchase behavior, and can see what products are under-represented in their assortment. They can then develop house brands, also known as private labels, to take advantage of these product opportunities. Amazon so far has launched private label brands in the apparel, consumer packaged goods (CPG), home and kitchen, and food categories. There are other brands that Amazon has registered trademarks for which have not yet launched.

- Continuing to expand their delivery infrastructure, with speculations that they will eventually no longer use Fedex and UPS as shipping carriers. In 2016 alone, Amazon purchased a cargo shipping company, launched Amazon One (the first of a fleet of 40 Prime-branded airplanes) and Amazon Flex (the "Uber of Amazon delivery"), purchased 4,000 truck trailers, and joined the FAA's drone advisory board, along with Facebook, Google, Boeing, Intel and UPS. In 2017, Amazon announced the 'Amazon Key' delivery system where consumers can install a keyless entry and monitoring system for Amazon deliveries and related services. The question that Jeff Bezos (Amazon's CEO) continually dodges is whether Amazon will ultimately use this delivery infrastructure purely for their own purposes, or eventually make a business from it — as was the case with the hugely profitable Amazon Web Services (AWS) business. I'm expecting to see this resolved one way or another in the next couple of years.

- Developing incremental changes and improvements to their paid search platforms. While Amazon's advertising platforms have attracted more attention and spend from all kinds of consumer product brands, their capabilities still lag behind the dominant players of Facebook and Google. At Bobsled Marketing we sometimes joke that Amazon's advertising platforms resemble Google Adwords circa 2004. However, Amazon is making fast strides in this area, launching new features in the past year including headline search ads.

- Continuing investment in hardware and the 'Smart Home'. In late 2017, Amazon launched six new Alexa-enabled Echo devices for the home, plus the Amazon Key delivery system and security camera. According to some, Amazon is winning the smart home race against Google and Apple, with brisk adoption of the Alexa voice system and new devices, including glasses, on the horizon. It's clear that Amazon sees voice-enabled commerce as the next wave of innovation beyond mobile commerce.

As you can see, there's a *lot* going on — and that's just the information that's been released (or uncovered). The opportunities are always expanding on Amazon, and so it's time to dive into how you can capitalize on those opportunities in your own company.

Chapter Two: The Expansion of Amazon

Amazon is one of the most powerful companies in the world today, and their pace is showing no sign of slowing down. They've quickly come to dominate the ecommerce space, and have even extended their reach into traditional retail businesses. These days, if you sell physical products, you can't afford *not* to be on Amazon. They are the most trusted platform in the world for online purchasing, and have market penetration that no business today — no matter how loyal their customers — can compete with.

As we begin, there are three key elements to understand about Amazon and why your brand should be on their platform. These factors apply to every kind of retail business, whether you have an ecommerce brand, an established brick and mortar retail business, or a product-based start-up.

1. **It's the biggest retailer in the world.**

Being on Amazon is like having a storefront in the most popular mall in the world. You can't beat the traffic, positioning and customer experience. For the 2017 holiday shopping season, 72% of shoppers planned to look for gifts on Amazon. Amazon was responsible for about 44% of all U.S. e-commerce sales in 2017, or about 4% of the country's total retail sales figure. Over 40% of purchase-related searches online now originate on Amazon, meaning that customers aren't even using Google any more to source their purchases — it's *all* happening through Amazon. It's the most obvious, high-traffic marketplace for any brand to be. Customers are ready and willing to buy there like nowhere else, and there is nothing else to *do* on the platform but shop (which sets it apart from Google, Facebook and even your own ecommerce store).

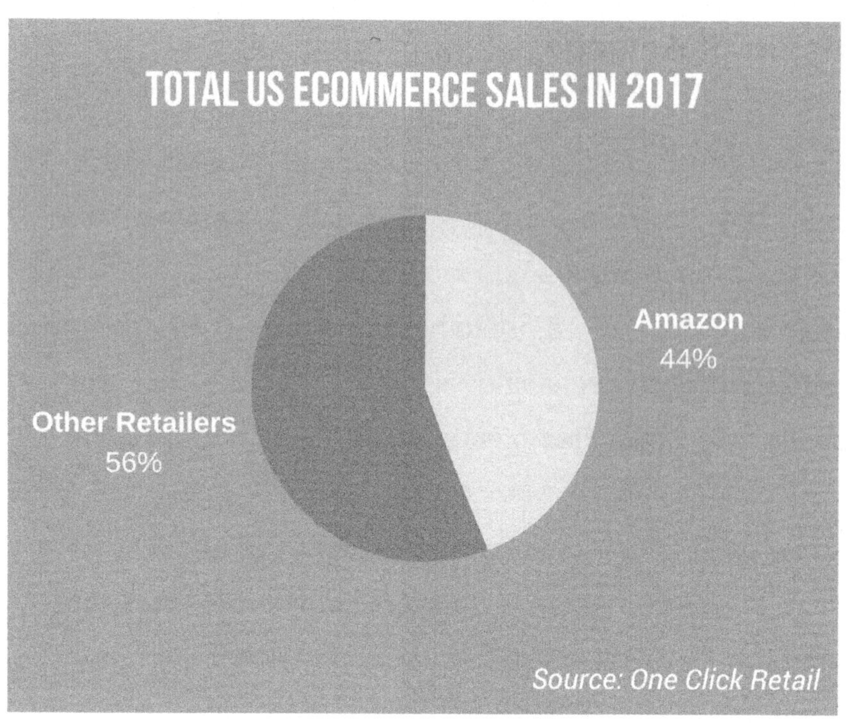

2. **If you don't list your products, someone else might.**

There's a misconception among consumers (and even some retailers) that only official brands are allowed to sell products on Amazon. However, the reality is that a cottage industry of resellers has sprung up (from stay-at-home-moms to large businesses), who purchase large quantities of products at a department store or from a retailer, then list these products for sale on Amazon to make money themselves. This is known as Retail Arbitrage and for some brands, it leads to serious reputational issues with consumers, and channel conflict with their other retail partners. With such low barriers to entry, Amazon has become a huge sales channel, so if someone sees an opportunity to sell your product, they will start doing so on Amazon. It's far better for you to be on the platform, controlling the conversation around your brand and selling your products, rather than giving up that control and revenue to someone who has no actual ties to your business.

3. **Their fulfillment capabilities are world-class.**

There are over 700 Amazon fulfillment centers worldwide. They have centers all over Europe, Asia and South America. Even if your company has a robust fulfillment system, with multiple fulfillment centers, warehouses and shipping arrangements, Amazon can augment your existing logistics capabilities. If you don't have an existing logistics capability, they can do *everything* for you. For example, we have a client who is a billion-dollar, household name company, with robust, well-established logistics capabilities. They've had decades to hone their fulfillment process, and they recently decided to outsource it all to Amazon. Instead of dealing with endless logistical details, they simply have their products sent directly from their manufacturers to Amazon's warehouses. Amazon has invested an enormous amount into their infrastructure, to the point where they are competing with stand-alone fulfillment businesses such as UPS and FedEx.

There is really no competition with Amazon when it comes to brand recognition, logistics operation, or business opportunity.

As a product-based brand, you can take advantage of this massive infrastructure and market penetration to expand the reach and revenue of your own business. Not only is there *current* market penetration, but the trends are showing that Amazon customers become more loyal over time, particularly among Prime members. According to research published by Consumer Intelligence Research Partners (CIRP) in October 2017, Amazon at that time had 90 million Prime members in the United States – over half of all households. Once Amazon Prime members renew for a second year, Amazon appears to have captured them for the long term. After a second year, renewal rates are over 95%, and have improved gradually in the past two years.

The reason why Prime members are so important to the ecommerce giant is quite simple: they spend more money on the platform than regular customers. According to CIRP, Prime members spend an average of $1,300 a year on Amazon, whereas non-members spend just $700. Even if you connected with just a tiny percentage of these 90 million super-users, it could transform your business.

Growth Predictions for Amazon To 2025

Amazon is investing heavily in international growth markets, as there's clear profit potential by reaching these emerging markets. This includes territories such as India, Latin America, and South-East Asia, where economies are growing, more and more people are coming online, and disposable incomes are gradually increasing. Amazon is also continuing to build out their infrastructure in Europe, and they are moving along a clear timeline of international expansion for their ecommerce arm.

As I mentioned in Chapter One, in the next few years Amazon is also likely to deepen their involvement in logistics, developing their capabilities to the point of becoming an alternate shipping carrier. Jeff Bezos has been asked the question repeatedly over the years as to whether his company will put UPS and FedEx out of business. The answer has always been 'no', but at a conference in early 2016 he did say that during holiday seasons, the shipping carriers have always let them down in their mission to provide exceptional customer service, and for that reason…

"We don't plan to replace UPS. We just plan to supplement their services… heavily."

And he means it. Amazon has been leasing aircraft, buying trailer trucks and even ocean shipping companies for their 'supplementation program' in order to meet the high demand and expectations of their customers.

Finally, they're going to move deeper into specific categories. For example, apparel has been held up as the 'last bastion' of traditional retail. Retailers insisted for years that people don't want to buy clothes online, wanting to try each piece on in-store, and that ecommerce would never fully meet the needs of the apparel markets. But Amazon has committed heavily to apparel, making the process seamless for consumers to purchase (and return) all kinds of clothing and launching several of their own private label apparel brands. The Echo Look acts as a virtual at-home dressing room experience complete with input from fashion stylists and the ability to suggest and order new clothing items and accessories. The bet has paid off, too — some analysts say that Amazon will soon overtake Macy's as the biggest clothing retailer in the US.

Another category that Amazon has invested heavily in is grocery and gourmet food. Like apparel, Amazon has been quietly creating its own private label brands of food products under such names as Happy Belly and Wickedly Prime for the past couple of years. New brick and mortar store concepts are being built and tested, including a "Just Walk Out" cashier-less convenience store concept, and a click-and-collect grocery store. If innovating in the category were not enough, Amazon acquired Whole Foods in mid-2017. Category by category, Amazon is making its presence felt.

The revenue potential with Amazon in the next five to 10 years is extraordinary. For retailers not yet selling on the platform, there's nothing but upside to getting involved. You get access to a *much* bigger market, you can ensure that your brand and products are being represented optimally online, and you can ensure a high level of customer satisfaction.

Amazon is not, however, a panacea. Listing on Amazon should not replace owning your own ecommerce platform. It's never wise to put all of your eggs in one basket, particularly with a platform that has been designed specifically to benefit the customer, not the seller. You generally won't be able to build a relationship with Amazon or their customers the way you can on your own platform. Like any business, it's important to have multiple sales channels to protect yourself and to ensure that your business remains healthy if one channel goes down. Listing on Amazon can be a powerful addition to your business, but don't rely on it as your sole source of revenue and growth.

Understanding Amazon As It Applies to *Your* Business

There are three main methods of selling available for retailers looking to expand their brand on Amazon. There's the Vendor Program, the Fulfilled By Merchant (FBM) Program and the Fulfilled By Amazon (FBA) Program. There's also the Launchpad program, which we'll cover. FBA tends to be more popular with ecommerce stores and start-ups, while the Vendor Program is generally used by large brands with traditional business models. The FBA and FBM models allow you to sell directly to the consumer via Amazon's platform and infrastructure, while the Vendor Program is essentially a wholesale model, where you deal with a buyer, ship in your inventory, and then let Amazon handle the rest.

FBM allows sellers to ship products to customers directly, for items purchased on Amazon. Established companies with existing fulfillment infrastructure might be drawn to this option, as it allows them to use their existing processes and put greater volume through their shipping providers. However, products which are Fulfilled By Merchant are not eligible for the Prime program, which puts many customers off buying their items — whatever savings you might make through shipping your own orders may be nullified by this lower sales volume. While on the surface, FBA might seem more expensive than your own fulfillment, consider the other soft costs with fulfilling customer orders — the labor and technology costs associated with customer service, handling return requests, tracking down issues with deliveries, the cost of warehouse space, labor costs for picking, packing and shipping orders, and so on. These are all handled by Amazon under the FBA and Vendor programs.

There is a new program called 'Seller Fulfilled Prime' which allows merchants to get Prime eligibility for their items, while fulfilling the order themselves. But the requirements are very high, given that you must provide the same level of service that Amazon does, including free returns and two-day shipping to customers. We created a detailed white paper about this program, available as a free download on our Resources Page (bobsledmarketing.com/amazon-expansion-plan-resources) for readers of this book. We don't cover the FBM model much further in this book, because I believe the cost:benefit ratio of using the FBA model usually wins out.

As in traditional retail, selling direct to the consumer on Amazon is generally more lucrative. Instead of giving the retailer a 50% discount, you get to keep the wholesale margin *and* the retail margin. That's why FBA is appealing to so many companies. Not only do they get to hand off logistics and fulfillment, but they also get to keep more of the total revenue. This frees them up to focus on growing their brand and looking after their customers. For large, well-established companies, the Vendor Program fits neatly with their existing infrastructure, and simply adds another high-volume sales channel to their business. They can increase their revenue without increasing their overhead. And finally, there is the option of combining both formats in a 'hybrid' model, where brands split their assortment across the Vendor and FBA platforms to maximize the benefits of both.

After working with over 100 businesses to expand their brands on to Amazon, we've found that there are three types of business that benefit most from adding Amazon's platform to their arsenal:

1. Direct-to-consumer brands
2. Established retail brands
3. Product-based start-ups

Making the Right Choice For Your Business: FBA, Vendor Program, Launchpad, or a Hybrid approach?

If you have a direct-to-consumer brand...

Most established ecommerce businesses that are looking to expand onto Amazon are focused on large-scale revenue growth. If you fit into this category, you might have a target operating margin that you are working towards, say in the region of 30%. This is the margin you would want to extract *after* paying for your inventory, covering the cost of selling online, and paying Amazon's fees. The ultimate goal here is revenue growth, but not to the detriment of profits.

Direct to consumer brands can fit into both the FBA Program and the Vendor Program, so it's important for you to assess which option is right for your particular business and priorities. A key advantage of the FBA Program is that it provides better margins for smaller companies that need the additional revenue. There are, of course, exceptions to this rule (heavy items or very inexpensive items are often unprofitable when sold on FBA), but you can control the price and you get to control your inventory.

With the Vendor Program, Amazon sets the selling price of your products. If they set the price lower than you would like, it can create conflict with your other sales channels, which we'll explore later in this book. The other issue is that they may not order inventory from you in an effective way — they might not order enough inventory because their prediction algorithm miscalculates demand, or they might not order all the sizes or variations you have available.

However, if you are prioritizing simplicity, streamlined processes and scale, the Vendor Program will usually be the better option. It saves you from having to handle customer service and inventory management, and doesn't require you to add any processes to your existing model.

Vendor Central has always been invite-only, and it does seem like fewer brands are being invited to the platform. Amazon is moving toward the self-serve model of Seller Central, constantly adding new features and education for Sellers. I'm sure that Amazon will always have some kind of wholesale program for brands, but there are less direct human contacts even within the vendor team. Some of our clients at Bobsled Marketing no longer have a human point of contact after many years of having a Vendor Manager or Buyer. The general trend is that Amazon ultimately prefers to automate and centralize its services, and vendor management appears to be no exception.

If you have an established retail brand…

For traditional retailers, the Vendor Program is often reassuringly familiar. All you have to do is monitor purchase orders, fill them on time, and then take your payment 90 days later. For large companies used to doing wholesale, it removes any concerns about having to deal directly with customers or complicating the processes that you've honed over a number of years.

The other advantage of the Vendor Program is that it's more suited to scale. The program has robust tools and capabilities to deal with catalogs that contain hundreds or thousands of SKUs. There's access to more detailed reporting, additional advertising options, and it allows big companies to implement a powerful extra arm to the business without adding significant complexity to the process.

You might be attracted to the Vendor Program because you don't do retail orders in your existing model, but you might be served just as well by the FBA program, particularly if you can't afford any channel conflict. For example, if you are selling to Best Buy, and *need* your product to be listed on Amazon for $30 in order to maintain a good relationship with Best Buy, FBA can give you that control. This allows you to get involved with selling on Amazon and stop leaving all those potential sales on the table, without damaging your existing business.

	FULFILLED BY MERCHANT (FBM)	FULFILLED BY AMAZON (FBA)	VENDOR
Selling Platform	Seller Central, also known as marketplace seller or 3rd party (3P).		Vendor Central, also known as 1st Party (1P).
Selling Model	Direct to consumer via Amazon's platform and infrastructure.		Wholesale Purchase Orders to Amazon.
Order Fulfilment	Merchant handles inventory warehousing, order fulfillment, and customer returns.	Amazon handles inventory warehousing, order fulfillment, and customer returns.	Amazon handles inventory warehousing, order fulfillment, and customer returns.
Prime Eligible?	No, but potential to enroll in Seller Fulfilled Prime.	Yes	Yes
Pricing	Amazon charges a 15% referral fee on sales in most categories. Seller covers cost of order fulfillment.	15% referral fee, plus FBA fulfillment fees.	Wholesale pricing. Can also include additional co-op, chargebacks, and other fees.

Image: A summary of the Vendor (wholesale) and Seller (marketplace) models on Amazon.

FBA functions as something of a halfway house between being a wholesaler and being a retailer. You get the improved retail margins, while enjoying the simplicity of a wholesale arrangement. All you have to do is send bulk quantities to Amazon's fulfillment centers and *they* take care of all the retail orders. It's the best of both worlds, although you do have to factor in customer support and a little more oversight of the channel.

There's a small monthly fee of $39.95 to sell on FBA, and in most categories in FBA you pay Amazon a 15% referral fee on each sale. Now, that's something you wouldn't be paying on your own ecommerce store, but you're also not paying for hosting, security, payment processing, fulfillment services, customer service… Amazon takes care of all that for you. The 15% fee could in fact be *less* than what you would be paying to handle it all yourself.

If you have a product-based start-up...

In this situation, you are most likely part of a new, fast-moving company whose priority is speed to market. You might have funding or you could be bootstrapped, but you're willing to try a new channel to increase your revenue and market share. You probably don't need too much market validation and understand the online consumer space enough to feel confident just committing to the platform. FBA is usually the best option here, for the same reasons that it works for established ecommerce businesses (you can set your prices, you get paid more regularly, and you get contact with your early customers), though you can also consider using Amazon's Launchpad platform.

Since introducing Launchpad in the US in 2015 and Europe in 2016, Amazon has been connecting hardware startups and hot new brands with successful crowdfunding campaigns to get them onto this new program. It describes itself as, "Unique and unexpected products from today's brightest startups", and when pitching companies on the benefits of the program Amazon says that it gives brands increased exposure and setup guidance.

Launchpad is run on the Vendor Express Platform - a streamlined, automated version of Vendor Express. Just like the full Vendor platform, this means potentially smaller margins than selling via the retail marketplace, and 60 or 90 day payment terms after filling your purchase orders (which can cause a cashflow issue for start-ups). We have found that there are serious limitations on the Vendor Express platform compared with Seller Central, and it's much more difficult to troubleshoot issues. New brands are required to send a quantity of free units for Amazon to test demand, before they will place actual purchase orders. This can result in a very slow start for brands on this platform, who often need to see results quickly.

However, you could also get some perks: The Launchpad marketing team will help you launch your product, they'll boost your listing with free product placements across the platform and on the Launchpad store front, your products can be enrolled in the Amazon Vine program, to ensure that you get plenty of reviews upfront (though you pay for this privilege), and you get custom product pages which can display more visual details. Still, there are many alternatives to these promotional features on the Seller Central platform which are explained later in the book.

How to Choose Between The Different Seller Programs:

If you decide against Launchpad, the alternatives are Seller Central or Vendor Central (if you receive an invitation). The Seller Central program is where a brand sells direct to customers, with Amazon taking a percentage referral fee — usually 15%.

You're given the option to have Amazon fulfill customer orders (FBA) or do fulfillment yourself. This option often results in a better profit margin for the brand, and the brand can set the selling price to the customer. Brands also have more control over their inventory levels and are able to change most details on their product page in real-time.

However, the brand will be responsible for more customer service activities, and some marketing tools like embedded videos and brand pages are not available to use.

If you have already launched and have a few channels working for you, FBA might be the better choice. It allows you to retain as much revenue as possible and keep your options open when it comes to selling your product at a price you're happy with. Ultimately, though, it comes down to the priorities and stage of your company:

- What is the average retail price of items in your core assortment? Your average retail price affects your potential margins on Amazon.

- Are your margins wholesale-friendly? Does your brand already have a wholesale program, or would your profit margins support it? A standard wholesale discount is 50% of the retail price (RRP / MSRP).

- How much control do you require over retail pricing? Some companies need more control over their pricing, to create a consistent experience for customers, and possibly also for wholesale relationships.

- Are your operations wholesale-friendly? Selling to Amazon as a Vendor means that you'll need to fill large Purchase Orders (PO's) and have them sent to Amazon from a warehouse in the US.

- How sensitive is your cash flow cycle? The frequency with which your company gets paid can have a big impact on your company's cash flow. Vendors get paid in 60 or 90 day terms, whereas on Seller Central your payment is every two weeks.

- What are your key marketing priorities? Is your company's primary focus on developing a brand and preserving control over your product listings, in keeping to a budget, or just making the most money possible?

A Hybrid Model

Some brands will benefit from using both the Vendor program as well as the FBA model. This can be the case where a brand already has a satisfactory relationship with Amazon on the Vendor side, but has found that Amazon is not purchasing all their SKUs, or in meaningful enough quantities to prevent sell-through.

If you have a Vendor account, you can then open an additional FBA account selling the same items (or some additional items) to cover you in case your Vendor stock sells through. Using a hybrid model will allow Amazon to list and fulfill all the units that they have in stock, while providing back-up inventory when/if there are any stock-outs of Vendor inventory.

Other benefits include:

- Minimize the level of customer service required by your brand, by having Amazon manage some products on Vendor Central.
- Some marketing tools are available only on Vendor Central. For example, being able to choose the time and day of Lightning Deals, the Vine Reviewer program, and product coupons. This is becoming less of a draw however - in 2017, Amazon made some promotional tools and advertising types available on Seller Central which were previously exclusive to the Vendors.
- Control pricing of their products on specific products. Seller Central allows a brand to set the price and only run sales when they want; whereas on Vendor Central, Amazon controls the price. As discussed earlier, this can lead to channel conflict for brands who sell through other retail channels. On Seller Central, brands can set their FBA merchandise at the correct MSRP, capturing more

margin on those SKUs than they would have achieved on Vendor-fulfilled SKUs, while maintaining price integrity.

- Brands can list new-to-market SKUs much faster than they could through the Vendor program. Amazon has to accept the new products and place a Purchase Order before the product can be made available on Amazon.

Putting this hybrid model in place will require both a Vendor Central or Vendor Express account, in combination with a Seller Central account.

Chapter Three: Selling on Amazon Compared To Traditional Retail

Selling to brick and mortar retail stores is a much more collaborative process than selling online. In traditional retail settings, you develop a working relationship with a buyer or team over time, improving the quality of that relationship as you prove that your company and your products are reliable. As time goes on, buyers from retailers will often start telling you the types of products they are looking for, promotions they have coming up that you can be part of, and even helping you with your assortment planning. You get to negotiate the terms of your agreement with them, such as when they pay you and the rates they give you. It's a give-and-take relationship that organically grows your business.

If you're dealing with large distributors like Walmart, though, they are going to control the relationship, and it's hard to develop any real leverage. They're always going to hardball you on your wholesale prices, charge you for premium placements in stores, and push you to provide discounts for coupons. It's an aggressive model that can be tough to deal with... but you can also reap the benefits of that relationship over the long term, because you also get access to hundreds of thousands — if not millions — of customers around the country.

The traditional model *is* changing, though. Brick and mortar retailers like Walmart, Best Buy and Target are expanding aggressively into ecommerce as well. Walmart acquired online retailer Jet.com for $3.3 billion in 2016, and has been playing a tit-for-tat game with Amazon to compete with the Prime membership program ever since.

While it seems unlikely that they'll have the same level of success that Amazon has achieved (since they're so late expanding into ecommerce), there's no reason that your products shouldn't be listed on their platforms as well. This is where dealing with the demanding brick and mortar retail relationship has the highest leverage, as having an existing relationship is going to make it easier to get set up on their new platforms.

Another type of retail relationship you might have is with distributors and resellers. Distributors could be selling to hundreds or thousands of mom-and-pop stores, international buyers and any number of online partners. In this situation, you have very little control over the final destination or buyers of your products. Even if you put in clauses dictating who and where the products can be sold, you'll never know if a purchaser is then on-selling the products after getting them from your distributor. You have very little control over that scenario, which is the advantage of selling on either of the Amazon programs: you have more control over the direct relationship with the customer, and how the product is communicated to them.

In the Vendor Central Program, the process is quite similar to the traditional brick and mortar model. You work with a buyer, you get to negotiate the terms, and they can be quite helpful in your assortment planning. The key difference is that you could potentially have more leverage with Amazon than you do with traditional retailers. If they push you too hard on price or terms, or spring unexpected return fees or co-op fees on you in the Vendor Program, you can simply switch to FBA.

(Note that the Vendor Central Program is not to be confused with Vendor Express — the more entry-level program — where a computer algorithm dictates the price, and you don't get any direct access to a Vendor Manager.)

On FBA, the key distinction from brick and mortar stores is that you get to control the inventory, price, and customer experience when they have a question about a product. Unless you have a store and platform of your own, there's no other place to sell where you would get this level of control.

Understanding these differences, then, you can see why it is so important to pick the right program for your brand. Channel conflict is a big issue for many retail brands: they've spent *years* building positive relationships with their distributors and buyers, and those relationships are real assets to the company as they grow. If a seller joins the Vendor Program, there is a risk that Amazon will price their items at a lower rate than their other retail partners sell for, which can jeopardize the relationships that they've worked so hard to build.

That's not to say that it's not worth the risk. In 2017, Amazon was scored by consumers as one of the top 5 most trusted companies in America. People love shopping there because they get free returns, they always get treated well, and if they ever have a problem with the product or seller, it's taken care of immediately. For sellers, it means that you can get sales from customers you couldn't have reached before, even through your own online store. It opens up a whole new market segment for you to sell into, despite being weighted in favor of the customer's experience over the seller's.

Balancing Amazon With Your Own Ecommerce Platform

Amazon gets *so* much traffic — the kind of traffic that would crush your ecommerce store if it suddenly came your way. Not only are hundreds of thousands of people using Amazon every day, but they already have their credit cards saved, they use one-click purchasing, and don't think twice about regularly buying stuff on Amazon. On your own store, your customers just won't have the same risk tolerance and willingness to buy, even if you're a well-known brand with good trust built up with your customers.

If you have an existing ecommerce store, you are already working on driving traffic to your store, whether with ads, search engine optimization (SEO) or content. You've got solutions in place for customer service, logistics and order fulfillment, handling returns, storage of inventory and so on. With all that already in place, adding Amazon to your arsenal can double your total online sales, without doubling your overhead.

Retaining Control of Your Brand Online

When you're selling to traditional brick and mortar stores, losing control of your brand is not a big risk. There might be the occasional rip-off artist that comes along, or you might not like how your products are displayed in stores, but there's rarely any serious cause for concern around the integrity of your brand.

Online, and particularly on Amazon, that risk does increase. Counterfeiting has become an issue for some brands on Amazon. This is because there are tools which will allow people to work out how much of a particular product is selling each month, thereby gauging the success of that product of Amazon. The barrier to entry is low for new sellers, so you do see opportunists taking advantage of that and starting to sell knock-off products.

The fact is that Amazon is a marketplace where anyone can sell goods they have legally acquired. Amazon's strategy is to offer the largest assortment of products, with the most convenient buying experience at competitive prices.

The Buy Box algorithm creates a pro-buyer environment. This is the way Amazon's system chooses which seller gets the sale in cases where multiple sellers are offering the same product:

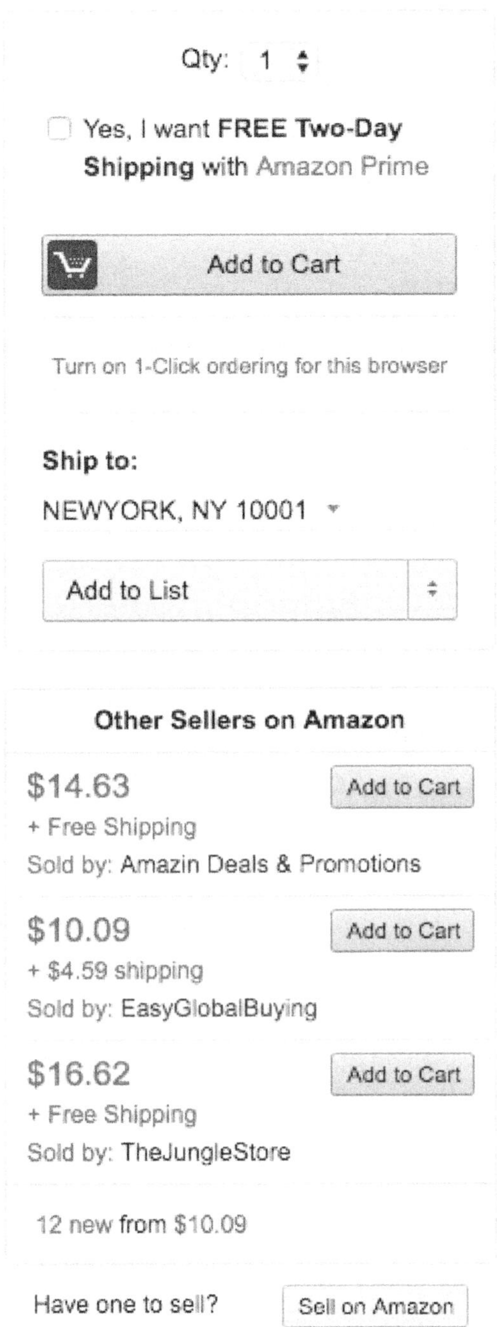

Above: a product with multiple Sellers who are "competing for the Buy Box".

As much as the price-reducing mechanism of having multiple sellers per product listing is helpful to Amazon and to customers, it does not favor sellers. While many sellers accept the rules of the game and strive to win the Buy Box algorithm, for others, the concept of the Buy Box creates a few sticking points:

- It generally drives down the price of their products. Having multiple sellers of a product often results in them having to compete on price. 'Repricing' software is often used by these sellers to automate the process of reducing prices of items to a fixed level in order to win the Buy Box and get the sale.

- Reduced prices may affect customer perception of the brand. If your brand has a strategic pricing model outside of Amazon's platform, it can be frustrating to have this undermined in such a significant market.

- Reduced prices affect relationships with other vendors. You might have a MAP (Minimum Advertised Price) policy in place with your other vendors, which might be completely ignored on Amazon by an anonymous seller. Brands who sell to retail stores or distributors might then find these relationships affected when other vendors see a price lower than the MAP listed on Amazon.

- Product pages that are off-brand. Anyone can create a new listing for your product if they have that product in stock in new condition, are eligible to sell in the category, and have an Amazon Seller Account. They may not have the correct product information or might be using a poor quality product photo, which in turn reflects poorly on the brand. Since there is little incentive to follow brand guidelines for the listing, this poor experience may take a toll on customer loyalty. This is frustrating for brands who have worked hard to develop consistency across their sales channels, only to have it undermined by rogue sellers.

So what does Amazon do to protect brands?

Amazon will take aggressive action against inauthentic products. For example, if someone is selling fake Sony Playstations as the real deal, the official seller can raise it with Amazon. From their perspective, fake products are absolutely unacceptable.

Understandably, Amazon doesn't want to be known as the 'Silk Road of ecommerce', so if they get claims about inauthentic products, they are very fast to remove them.

Beyond dealing with obviously fake products, though, there are several strategies you can use to protect your brand on Amazon.

1. Understand that Amazon will not help you take down unauthorized sellers.

Amazon *wants* to have multiple sellers of each product, because it helps to keep prices competitive, making the products (and the overall marketplace) all the more appealing to buyers. Requests for Amazon to help police your brand will fall on deaf ears, even if you have protective assets like a patent or trademark. Amazon does not view unauthorized sellers (i.e. anyone but you and your authorized distributors) as policy violators. Amazon is a catalog business which is designed for more than one seller to be on an individual listing. Only counterfeit items are against Amazon's sales policy.

2. Apply for the Amazon Brand Registry

Brand Registry is a program that is fairly easy to enroll in if you're the manufacturer or an OEM (original equipment manufacturer) of a branded product. Your enrollment ensures that other sellers cannot easily make changes to your product detail page. It is an important way of ensuring that your product pages are represented correctly, but doesn't prevent other sellers from listing your product. It also certifies you as the brand owner which gives you important brand control tools, including:

- Exemption from having to use UPCs to list your products
- Priority "content contribution". The copy, keywords and other product listing content you submit will override any content that other Sellers try to submit.
- Faster reporting of counterfeiters and trademark violations. Sellers can file copyright and trademark infringements against multiple listings using the tool.

In addition to the brand control features, Brand Registry also gives brands access to optimization tools like Enhanced Brand Content (more visually compelling product pages), the ability to build a multi-page storefront allowing you to enhance your brand story with video, more content and additional images, and the ability to create headline search ad campaigns in addition to regular sponsored products ad campaigns.

Please note that this presupposes the brand is registered properly, and that every product has been correctly enrolled, including Manufacturer Part Number and UPC codes if applicable.

(Enrolling in the Brand Registry may also cause Amazon to categorize your brand as 'protected', meaning that other Sellers must first get authorization to sell your brand, and potentially even pay a processing fee of up to $2,000 for the privilege. This new program was rolled out in August 2016, and at the time of writing, details were still scant about which brands are selected for this program. This update could potentially change the landscape for sellers, but too much is unknown at this stage for me to include any more commentary around the program than this. See our Resources Page (http://www.bobsledmarketing.com/amazon-expansion-plan-resources) *for the most up-to-date information on this program.)*

3. Keep your brand identity front and center

Maintain a public website for your brand for which you can prove ownership — this is actually a requirement for applying to the Amazon Brand Registry. You should also have your brand name printed on the packaging and the actual product. This is another requirement of the Brand Registry process, but will also help in identifying counterfeit items (see below).

4. Include exclusivity and MAP policies in your distributor contracts

Execute iron-clad agreements with distributors, resellers or retailers who may sell your product, explicitly preventing them from selling your brand on Amazon themselves, or requiring them to adhere to your MAP policy if preferred. Further protection can also be found by serializing your products. If you encounter reselling issues, serialization allows you to find out which distributor is not playing by the rules. If you find that wholesale distributors are ignoring the exclusivity or MAP clause, you can then choose to take further action which could include raising their wholesale price so that it's financially untenable for them to continue undercutting you on Amazon. Enforcing exclusivity contracts is just as important as setting them up, and you'll want to be tracking who is selling your products on a regular basis, so you can nip any untoward behavior in the bud.

5. Handle unauthorized Amazon resellers reactively

One way we do this for Bobsled Marketing's clients is to proactively monitor product pages and accounts to identify when products have unauthorized Amazon sellers. When we identify such products, we have a two-step process to handle the issue:

- Send a 'cease and desist' style message through the Amazon system directly to the other seller. This eliminates a good percentage of unauthorized sellers.

- If we believe it is a counterfeit item, we may place a 'test buy' to validate. After verifying that the product is not authentic, we file a complaint with Amazon and try to have the seller's offer taken down. You will not get any compensation from Amazon for doing this.

6. Don't use stickerless commingled inventory when using the Amazon FBA program.

When you sign on to FBA, there is an option available to *not* apply Amazon barcode labels (stickers) to your inventory when it's shipped in. However convenient it might seem, do not use this option. This means your product can be mixed in with potentially counterfeit items and can create a host of problems down the line, which we'll explore in more detail shortly.

7. Consider becoming an Amazon Vendor.

We have already discussed using Seller Central compared to Vendor Central (which basically comes down to the difference between selling on Amazon directly to their customers, or selling to Amazon on a wholesale basis). One other benefit of being a Vendor on Amazon is that you will become the defacto brand owner on Amazon. It will then be extremely difficult for other sellers to make changes to your product detail page, such as changing the product description and product images, adding new variations, and other unwelcome changes.

Because counterfeiting and phoney sellers (those who set up Seller Central accounts, make a couple of sales, then close their accounts before ever shipping product) have emerged as a serious reputational issue for Amazon, they are investing in new technology and programs to address these issues. One new program is called "Transparency", where merchants can add a QR-type barcode to their inbound inventory, which both Amazon and the end customer can scan to confirm whether the product is genuine.

Here are the answers to the most common questions we get, following on from these seven strategies:

Q: As a foreign brand, should I set up a US entity to help protect my brand?

A: I advise against setting up a US entity simply for the purposes of policing your brand, as it won't necessarily be effective. Some of these unauthorized sellers won't be US companies either, so it won't necessarily be easy to enforce legal action. By setting up a US entity you'll also need to start dealing with all the paperwork, legal and tax affairs required of US companies.

Q: Will a trademark or patent help?

A: Trademarking your product and brand name, as well as acquiring design patents can be prudent and will give you more grounds for legal action in a 'worst case' scenario.

But it is difficult to actually obtain the identity of many sellers on Amazon, so you may never even get to the point of being able to pursue legal action.

Q: Is it possible to block other sellers on my product pages?

A: At the time of writing, Amazon has put in place protections for *some* brands selling on Amazon, but not all. You should put the above protections in place, but you'll need to also supplement that with ongoing monitoring of your product pages and react to any new, unauthorized sellers. This is something we do daily or weekly for Bobsled Marketing clients, because it's such an important factor in maintaining the quality of your listings.

Q: I have a MAP policy in place — shouldn't that protect me?

A: Amazon does not care about MAP, and they will do nothing to enforce it. The only real option to determine if any of your distributors are violating MAP is to introduce serialization to your product line. Also remember that from a legal standpoint, MAP is a concept that is only really used in the USA. Outside the USA such practices are generally considered price fixing.

***

Clearly, Amazon is not a 'set and forget' platform. You need to monitor your listings and competitor's listings in order to keep on top of your brand integrity. It's an understandable concern for brands, but ultimately Amazon is a high-reward platform if you are willing to tolerate a little bit of risk.

Understanding, then, that this is how Amazon is set up, your best option is to work closely with your distributors to ensure that all parties are protected and that an official seller will naturally win the sale. As we touched on earlier, this is known as 'winning the buy box', which is how Amazon distributes sales among the various sellers. We are going to delve into this in detail later on in the book, but rest assured that there are strategies you can use to bring your listing to the top of the seller selection for each of your products, and that optimizing those strategies will help you to win more sales and beat out other competitors.

Chapter Four: Logistical FAQs For Getting Started

Here at Bobsled we work with dozens of brands every year, and as each business starts expanding their presence on Amazon, some of the same questions crop up again and again. In this chapter, we're going to address the most common questions, as well as looking at a few misconceptions (and even some hidden benefits) about selling on Amazon.

The businesses we work with are at varying levels of their growth. For some companies, we come in right at the beginning, helping them set everything up from scratch. For others we come in when they've already got an account with Amazon US, and just need help with optimization, or when they are an established Amazon seller and are ready to set up and optimize their paid advertising efforts with Amazon's Pay-Per-Click (PPC) advertising platform. Finally, for some clients we manage their expansion into Amazon's international markets. The questions you'll see here, then, are reflective of the conversations we have across varying levels of business development. Some of these stages won't apply to you (either because you're not at that stage yet, or you've already surpassed it), so feel free to focus your attention on the questions and solutions that are most pertinent to your brand at the moment.

We need to consider the defensibility of our brand. How does Amazon factor into that?

There's no magic bullet when it comes to building a defensible business, and adding another sales channel is no exception, even when it's as big as Amazon. Guy Kawasaki, a legend in the marketing space, believes that defensibility in any business boils down to a few key things:

> *"Understand that very few companies are truly defensible for reasons other than because they either achieved critical mass or had a nine-month head start. You have domain expertise, connections, and what you're doing is hard. You're not*

the only team that can do this, but you're in a better position than most. You believe that you can build a business better than anyone." (source)

That said, Amazon can add significant velocity to your business: it helps to build your brand by getting your products in front of more people, and can help to boost your chances of getting into big-box retail if your listings perform well. If your competitors aren't doing Amazon well, or aren't using it to expand into new territories, then you gain a competitive advantage and potentially *years* of head start into untapped markets.

However, your performance does become more visible to competitors and potential copycats, and Amazon themselves can end up being a competitor by releasing private label versions of your product (though you should remember that this can happen with any traditional retailer such as private label products at Target, Walmart and the like). As I said, there's no magic bullet and you should view Amazon as a tool in your arsenal, rather than as a golden goose to be relied on over every other channel.

FBA seems like a great solution, but we're going to have a lot of moving parts in our logistics if we add another fulfillment program. Can Amazon help with that?

For many Amazon sellers, it comes as a pleasant surprise to discover that the FBA program will also let you fulfill sales orders from other platforms. Yes — Amazon will deliver sales you made through other marketplaces. You might have an online store, an eBay account and multiple marketplace listings... and they can all be shipped from Amazon to the end customer regardless of which platform the order actually came from. The fulfillment fees are slightly higher with that program than with regular FBA (you're using their infrastructure without them getting their usual 15% referral fee), but it's often worth the higher fees not to have to deal with multiple fulfillment solutions.

In fact, some brands use the FBA program as their *only* fulfillment solution. It's a little more expensive than using the more traditional carriers, but for many companies it's worth it, particularly if there has been a disappointing or difficult relationship with the original fulfillment provider.

What you can't do is to use Amazon as a fulfillment center with no restriction. In reality, you have a limit on how much inventory you can store at Amazon (especially when you first start selling). They don't want inventory sitting around for years if it's not going to sell. The storage space is costly to build and maintain, so Amazon has some protocols in place to control this issue. The Help section of Seller Central states that, *"Typically, inventory storage limits apply to new FBA sellers and existing FBA sellers with slower-moving inventory. We may also create storage limits for specific ASINs (Amazon Specific Identification Numbers)."*

You will usually start out with inventory limits that are only increased once you've sold through 8% or more of your available inventory over a nine-week period — therefore proving to Amazon that you have products which turn over adequately enough for them to 'invest' in storing it at their facilities.

Amazon will also charge you hefty storage fees if your products sit in their warehouses for more than six months. It is in your interest, then, not to send them too much stock up front. Obviously, you want to send them enough to meet demand — if you run out, every day out of stock is a day of lost revenue — but you don't want to have so much stock there that you get penalized. And before you think that it might be worth just eating the cost of the penalties, understand that they are very steep. In February and August of every year, Amazon conducts an Inventory Cleanup, at which time inventory units that are aged between six and 12 months are charged a Long-Term Storage Fee of $11.25 per cubic foot, and units that are aged over 12 months are charged a Long-Term Storage Fee of $22.50 per cubic foot.

This is compared with the fairly low storage rate of $0.69 per cubic foot per month from January to September and $2.40 per cubic foot per month from October to December.

As you can see, it's really important to get your stock levels right to maintain a healthy balance with Amazon's systems.

Can selling on Amazon cause conflict with my other sales channels?

We covered this in the last chapter as well, but it bears repeating that this is an important element to manage, particularly if your brand is relatively new. Channel conflict arises primarily with existing retail partners and distributors, usually only when you are using the Vendor Program and have relinquished control of how Amazon prices your products. You can see internal channel conflict as your own store can be cannibalized by your Amazon listing if it's at a lower price. That's a double whammy, because people are buying on Amazon where you probably have a lower margin, they're not becoming repeat visitors to your store, they're not making incidental or additional purchases, and you can't collect their email addresses to remarket to them.

For large, established retail brands that have long-standing retail relationships, channel conflict is often less of a concern — they know that things will balance themselves out eventually. However, for small companies who have been working night and day to establish retail relationships, it can be a cause for concern. That's why FBA is such an appealing option for so many businesses: it allows them to take advantage of Amazon's platform and visibility, without losing control of the pricing structure. They get all the benefits of a new market to sell into, without damaging the relationships that built their original markets.

We sell exclusively through ecommerce at the moment, and we're interested in getting into physical stores. Ignoring potential channel conflict, is it helpful or harmful to be on Amazon if you're trying to get your products into brick and mortar stores?

An interesting fact that has emerged from retail consultants that we partner with is that while you'd imagine stores don't want products to be on Amazon (so they have exclusivity and to avoid having customers price-checking in-store), a lot of buyers at big retail stores *want* to see a new brand on Amazon. A new brand is an unknown quantity for a retailer, so a presence on Amazon helps them to establish a sales history of that brand and validates the market demand for the product.

But retailers aren't just looking for the number of products you've sold. They need to see some good margins, good reviews, uniqueness in your products, and to know that you're prepared for retail (such as back-end programs, sales materials, retail packaging, etc) which is done upon presenting the products.

If you've got big plans for your brand and want to get it into big-name retail stores, getting it up and performing well on Amazon can improve your chance of getting it into these stores and making sure you get favorable deal terms. Ideally though, if your plan is to expand into brick and mortar retail, you would be using the FBA program on Amazon (over the Vendor or Launchpad programs) so that you can control the pricing and will be able to be competitive and appealing when you're dealing with retail buyers.

As an aside, we've seen new businesses (with what would otherwise be "slam-dunk" products) get crushed on Amazon because of some initial bad reviews due to shipping, rushed quality, and so on. Amazon should *not* be the initial testing ground for your minimum viable product — you can't remove bad reviews and it can be very difficult to repair your rankings. Not only does this damage your performance on Amazon, but it can prevent you from getting into retail stores down the line as well. As with any business, it's important to approach each new stage of your business growth strategically, so that you set yourself up for as much success and opportunity down the line as possible.

We've heard that Amazon can be a difficult retail partner for sellers. Is that true?

Amazon's unique selling proposition (USP) is that all they care about is providing the best possible experience to customers. They are obsessed with this mission, and everything in their business is secondary — including making things easy on their sellers. They refuse to do anything that will annoy customers, or make it less likely for them to return and shop again, and it makes sense, since the customers are where the money comes from. Amazon turns incredible amounts of revenue thanks to this approach. They're worth over $700 billion, and they consistently have the highest share prices and returns in the tech industry, with only Apple and Facebook performing at comparable levels. So yes, Amazon is extremely customer-centric, and sellers need to understand that they are not the platform's priority.

One example of this is the returns policy. Amazon offers easy returns, and it's a major point of appeal among consumers. Unfortunately, there is a loophole in the returns system that can be abused: If a customer wants to return something, they have to choose from a selection of reasons why. It might be that they ordered the wrong size, found it cheaper somewhere else, *or* that the item is defective or doesn't work. While there are multiple reasons available to explain why they are returning the item, this last one is the only option that allows them to avoid paying for the return shipping.

This allows people to return items for free (whether they're actually defective or not), meaning the seller gets hit with a return fee, and the item is marked as defective and therefore must be removed from Amazon's warehouse for inspection. If you have too many orders come back for this reason, Amazon will make an executive decision that the product is defective and shut your listing down. The number that will trigger this decision will depend on the category and type of product in question. In apparel, return rates could be around 25%, whereas some categories don't see a return rate much higher than 1-2%, so it really depends on what Amazon perceives to be a reasonable rate of return for your category. There's little recourse for this, and at this point, Amazon doesn't seem to be making it a priority to close this loophole, though there was a report that recently suggested that some consumers are having their accounts cancelled because their return rates are too high when compared to the return rates of similar products.

In some ways, Amazon can be more difficult than other retail partners. There are risks like this on the platform (as with any sales channel), but we would argue that the profit potential and brand expansion are worth it: if you're serious about growing a consumer retail brand, you have to be on Amazon to stay competitive. You just have to be diligent and proactive with your customer care and marketing strategies.

Do I have to have a US business entity to sell on Amazon US? Do I need international entities if I want to sell in international Amazon marketplaces? And what are my tax obligations?

You can register on Amazon US as an individual or a company, and you don't have to have a business entity set up… but that does not mean that you don't have any tax obligations. Unfortunately, these are pretty complex for ecommerce businesses, and it's *very* important that you find a tax accountant familiar with ecommerce to help you get this right. The United States sales tax system was originally designed for brick and mortar businesses like stores and restaurants where merchants would collect sales tax from each patron or customer — it was pretty simple.

The rapid uptake of ecommerce means that buyers and sellers are frequently not located in the same State. This means that the onus is on the seller to determine whether they are liable to collect and pay sales tax on each purchase, based on the buyer's shipping address and if the business has a presence in that State (which constitutes a "tax nexus"). A presence could include an office, warehouse, employees, or contracted agents. And most importantly for merchants, owning inventory in any particular State often creates a "tax nexus" for your business, meaning that you must start collecting and remitting tax on sales to customers in that State.

Each State has its own rules. Some have a sales tax provision and others don't, some specifically exclude Third Party Fulfillment Providers (3PLs) from their definition of a tax nexus, and some States have specific tax rates at the county-level. The trouble for Amazon FBA sellers is that they don't have a lot of control over where their inventory is held. Amazon determines where your inventory should be routed to, within the dozens of Fulfillment Centers around the country. Suddenly, Sellers could have inventory in 15 or 20 States right out of the gate and by default, be required to start collecting and remitting the applicable sales tax to each State.

If you do not have a US business entity, then any income from Amazon US sales will be taxed in your home country, and you may still be obligated to pay US sales tax. The good news is that there is now software that can automate the process of collecting and remitting sales tax in each of the jurisdictions where you have a tax obligation. The two best software options at the time of writing were TaxJar and Avalara.

The Federal income tax applies to foreign sellers when you're "engaged in a trade or business in the United States". That is a pretty broad definition, especially for companies whose only link to the US is that they ship inventory to an Amazon warehouse to be sold to customers in America. Some tax advisors take the position that if you don't have any staff in the US, and your only connection to the US is a third party independent contractor (such as Amazon, an independent distributor, or other independent contractor), it could be argued that this agent is not dependent on your company; therefore you are not engaged in a US trade or business and not subject to US taxation. However, other professionals take the position that since you are selling "regularly and continuously" to customers in the United States with inventory owned by you within the USA, you are "engaged in a US trade or business" and subject to US tax.

Now there is some good news for companies located in Tax Treaty Countries such as Australia, the UK, and much of continental Europe. Federal income tax is only applicable for you if you have to have a physical presence in the US with employees. Mario Lucibello, a Certified Public Accountant who specializes in this area, suggests that companies collect and file sales tax at a minimum. Most States have clear definitions of what constitutes a tax nexus, and often that includes if inventory is held in their state.

Now, if you are not incorporated, you *can* be held personally liable if you do not meet your tax obligations. The IRS is one of the most aggressive tax offices in the world, so it's worth getting this right first time around. Some sellers take a relaxed attitude and decide to deal with the consequences if they get caught, but that's a high risk. Admittedly, you may never have an issue, but if you do, it can wreak havoc on your business and your personal finances.

Much of the tax law is not really set up for use in the ecommerce world, and so it's a complex area that you need to get good guidance on. We are not tax experts, and we don't provide any tax advice, but we can recommend experts we work with regularly if you visit http://www.bobsledmarketing.com/amazon-expansion-plan-resources.

What's the timeline for getting accounts set up on Amazon US and other Amazon territories?

The first thing to realize is that you need to be approved by Amazon before you're allowed to sell in some categories. That includes food and groceries, beauty, jewellery and clothing. Food and beauty are regulated by the FDA. There are genuine health and safety issues that go with those categories, so Amazon wants to validate where your products are coming from. You have to produce at least two commercial purchase orders from your supplier or manufacturer, showing your orders to verify that you are actually doing business with a reputable manufacturer.

In the clothing category, they want to verify that you will provide quality items via quality listings, and that you're not going to be listing a single item or a few pieces out of your wardrobe. They want to see sellers that have a full catalog with multiple SKUs and are going to be worth their time. Jewellery is very restrictive, particularly when it comes to fine jewellery. Anything with precious stones or precious metals has an extremely strict appraisal process, and they also have ongoing laboratory tests that ensure you are compliant with their regulations.

You can't sell just anything on Amazon, either. In some categories, you really need to prove yourself to them — and you have to be prepared to go through fairly rigorous scrutiny to get your products approved. Taking that into consideration, if you're selling in a restricted category, you should add a couple of weeks (up to a couple of months) to your timeline to start making sales on Amazon. For this reason, we recommend that you start the submissions process well before you *need* the sales that you expect to generate from Amazon.

Otherwise, if you are in a non-restricted category, you could set up an account within 20 minutes or so. The next major step is listing your product catalog, so if you only have a couple of products to sell, that won't take very long to set up. If you have hundreds or thousands of SKUs, you'll probably be integrating your Amazon account with your inventory management software, so that could take a little longer, but this timeline depends largely on the software you're using and the number of products to be added.

The next major step is sending your inventory to Amazon. If you're using UPS to send smaller parcels to them individually, and depending on which fulfillment center you're sending to, you can probably have your inventory to Amazon's warehouses, and processed by Amazon to be made available for sale, within a week. It does depend on the time of the year — during the holidays the warehouses get very busy and take longer to receive items.

If you're sending by truck (either LTL or FTL — 'Less Than Load' or 'Full Truck Load'), those deliveries will need to be scheduled by the driver with Amazon. Amazon is very strict on the vehicles that comes into the delivery zones: they *must* be on time or will be rescheduled (and waiting for truck loads to be redelivered to Amazon can take up to a few weeks). Once it's been received and processed at Amazon, it will be made available for sale and will be discoverable by customers. In theory, you could have it done in a week if you had a dream run, but realistically you should allow a month or more as a margin of safety.

(When you are first getting set up, don't worry about optimizing all your product listings and making every page look perfect. Just get the basics built, because you can go back and update the listings later on, once your products have been dispatched to Amazon for processing. You'll have at least a few days between sending them off and the products becoming available, so it's more effective to spend the time at the beginning of the process actually getting inventory ready for shipment, and then using the interim time to optimize the listings as best you can, which we will discuss in the next part of the book.)

Something that you need to factor into your timeline is that Amazon also has its own barcode system, called FNSKU. (The FNSKU is an acronym for Fulfillment Network SKU or Fulfillment Network Stock Keeping Unit. The FNSKU is the way that Amazon identifies a product as unique to the seller that has sent it to the Amazon fulfillment center.)

Amazon can receive items that have a UPC barcode on them, but they will want to code that product into their system using their own barcodes. In the Amazon warehouses, a lot of things are automated. Robots are often scanning items and can only work with one barcode system. In the warehouse environment, then, if something has a barcode on it, it needs to be covered by an Amazon replacement. The decision you need to make here is whether you let Amazon barcode the products when they arrive at the warehouse, which can take a few more days, or whether you should apply Amazon's barcodes to your products yourself.

It's my strong recommendation that wherever possible, your company should label your inventory yourselves. We've seen several instances of Amazon applying the wrong barcodes to products, which creates an enormous chain reaction of problems: the customers get the wrong products, so you get a spate of returns saying the product is not what they ordered, then the listing can get shut down — all because of a mistake an Amazon robot made. Getting reimbursement for this kind of thing is like pulling teeth, and can jeopardize all the work you've done to get to this point.

Putting Amazon's labels on yourself, at either your storage facility or your manufacturing facility, is much better. It saves some money (Amazon charges twenty cents per unit to apply their barcodes, which can really add up for a large shipment), it speeds up the receiving time, and if you trust your own fulfillment center, then the chances are good that they will do a better job than Amazon will.

I'm shipping inventory from outside the US. Are there any other logistical considerations I need to take into account?

I'll outline the exact process for this in a moment, but first, two things to mention: your inventory set-up time may be longer if you're shipping your inventory in by sea. Expect the process to take at least a few weeks. Second, it's very much in your best interest to engage a freight forwarder to handle the logistics of the delivery, and a customs broker to get your products through customs. If your shipment gets to Amazon with duties or taxes still payable on it, they will not pay it. They will reject the delivery, and the whole shipment will be sent back to you at an exorbitant cost. The freight and customs clearance timelines are really the only thing that elongate the process of shipping inventory into the US, so you want to minimize the opportunities for this to drag on. It's critical that you have someone there on the ground to make sure things go smoothly at the customs port or border.

Finding a customs broker you can build a relationship with is very valuable. In this situation, your freight forwarder is also a critical player, as they will handle the scheduling of your shipment to be received at Amazon. Most freight forwarders are now familiar with Amazon's delivery requirements, but you should absolutely double check this before hiring your provider. If products are small and light and you're only sending a small quantity, you can use air freight with companies such as DHL and FedEx. Those companies usually provide end-to-end solutions, taking care of the customs brokerage and all the delivery logistics.

Here is a complete overview of the process for importing your inventory into the US for distribution on Amazon:

- Create the product listings on Amazon. You'll need to complete this step in order for Amazon to generate shipping information, including which FBA warehouses your products should be sent to.

- Prepare a commercial invoice, which includes the Importer of Record (IOR). The IOR can be the owner, purchaser, an authorized agent, or a licensed customs broker.

- Choose a customs broker. Some shipping carriers like FedEx and DHL offer this as part of their service, which can simplify things significantly. Brokers are the only people authorized to represent you in clearing imported goods through customs. If you don't want to use your shipping carrier as your broker, you can find one in the Ports section of the U.S. Customs and Border Protection website.

- Use a shipping carrier or freight forwarder to:
    - Ship the products from the factory or warehouse to the port.
    - Clear the products through customs for export.
    - Ship products to the destination port and offload them.

- Clear the products through customs for import. Your customs broker (or shipping carrier or freight forwarder if they offer this service) will handle this for you. Note:
    - Import duty and taxes are due when importing most items into a country. Check with the U.S. Customs and Border Protection to confirm the details for your shipment ahead of time.
    - There may be import restrictions and rules for your product: Agencies such as U.S. Department of Agriculture (USDA), U.S. Food and Drug Administration (FDA), and U.S. Consumer Product Safety Commission

(CPSC), among others may require a permit, license, or other certification, depending on what is being imported.

- Optional step: send products to a pre-fulfillment facility. This is a specialist company which prepares your items for sale on Amazon, including packaging the items according to Amazon's requirements, applying barcode labels, etc.

- Send products onto an Amazon fulfillment center. The specific fulfillment center which your goods are sent to will be specified when you create the products and shipment in Amazon's system.

This is obviously a fairly involved process. It's complex and costly, so if you're going to do it, it's worth getting it right first time around and engaging the right partners. We have several trusted partners we collaborate with who ensure that the import and delivery process runs like clockwork for our clients, listed on our Resources Page (bobsledmarketing.com/amazon-expansion-plan-resources).

Can I choose where Amazon sends my inventory?

Amazon has over 100 fulfillment centers around the US, but unfortunately, you don't get to choose the center your inventory goes to… even if your inventory is stored just down the road from one of them. Companies always want to send inventory to a single fulfillment center, but when you make your shipping plan (how many of each SKU you want to send), Amazon decides how many of those units goes to selected fulfillment centers. This decision is based on projected demand in different parts of the country, fulfillment center capacity, and other logistics factors.

Amazon will often split up the shipment and direct inventory to different fulfillment centers, and you will have to handle that distribution. This can be an issue for some companies, as it costs more money to send it three ways instead of one. There *is* the Inventory Placement Service, where you can tell Amazon that you just want to send your inventory to one fulfillment center, but even then you can't choose which one it will be. You also have to pay a fee per unit if you use this service, which can add up for a high-quantity shipment.

(One tip on this: inbound shipments can be cancelled after they are initially created, so it's possible to see where Amazon is likely to direct your inventory, without committing to actually sending anything in.)

We've listed our products, but we're not seeing any sales yet. What gives?

Another common misconception is that you can just throw up your product listings in whatever format you have them on your ecommerce store or eBay, and that people will find them and buy them. The truth is that you need to do a lot of optimization and careful development of your listings if you want to get traction on Amazon's platform. The only exception here is if your company is a household name, but even then, you'll see better performance when you take the time to get your listings right.

If it's a new product or new brand, or even something that is simply unknown in some households, then you need to get to understand the three tenets of the Amazon search system: relevance, sales velocity and conversion rate (discussed in detail in Chapter Four). These elements allow people to find your product, and for you to show them a compelling enough offer for them to want to buy. You've got to put in the work, just like you would on any other channel. Amazon is not a set and forget platform.

Someone else is selling our stuff without permission! What can we do?

We've covered this in depth earlier in the book, but again — one of the biggest misconceptions for businesses expanding onto Amazon is about who is allowed to sell what when it comes to your brand and products. As we discussed, unless your brand is restricted by Amazon, there's often nothing you can do with this problem but to manage it. Even if you do get the offending Seller taken down, it might be a temporary solution — more may pop up in time and you'll have to deal with the process all over again. It's just the cost of doing business on an open, high-visibility platform. Your best option is to ensure that your listings are fully optimized, provide the best possible customer service, and make sure you've got the three search elements handled so you can win the Buy Box as often as possible to beat out any competitors. You also need to be taking action against unauthorized sellers *daily*, until they get the message and take down their listings. This can be time-consuming and tedious, so this is something we do in-house for all our Bobsled Marketing clients.

We want to list all our product variations separately, so that we dominate the search results whenever someone searches in our category. What's the best way to do that?

Well, the best way is *not* to do that. It's a great idea in theory, but in reality, some variations of your product will perform much better than others. When you then factor in all the effort that goes into getting reviews, optimizing the on-page content for conversions, fostering healthy traffic to the page, getting your SEO right… it's much more difficult to get the same momentum across 10 different product pages than it is to get it for one product page. My philosophy is that you want all the variations of each product to be listed on the same page. It might be organized by size, color, scent, bundles, or quantity, so that the products that are doing really well can create a halo effect for the other variations.

Something else to understand is that listing your variations on the same page won't prevent a particular variation from showing up in the search results. For example, even if your red t-shirt is your best-selling item, having a blue variation listed on the same page will still show up when someone searches for ‘blue t-shirt’. The blue variation will show in the results, and when they click on the page, the blue variation will be displayed. Amazon’s search algorithm is very sophisticated — the most relevant variation will be the one that shows up, regardless of what other options you have listed on the page.

Chapter Five: Operations and Customer Support

Amazon is obsessed with their customers. They have a 24-hour service level agreement to maintain their high standards. No matter what timezone you're in, or which Amazon marketplace you're in, you are required to respond to all customer service queries within 24 hours. If you don't respond within that 24-hour timeline, it will affect your seller rating, which in turn impacts buyer confidence. And if you're competing with other sellers on your products, you may also see a decrease in how often you are winning the buy box. It's very important to maintain a good seller rating, as in addition to contributing to your positioning and sales, it can also qualify you for special programs and promotions that Amazon has.

Over the holidays, Amazon wants you to respond to customers within *12 hours.* It doesn't appear to affect your seller rating in quite the same way, but making customers wait during a high-stress time of year can provoke bad reviews (which, in turn, can produce the same damage to your seller rating).

The standard 24-hour response rate is always in play. 24 hours a day, seven days a week, even during holidays… there are no exceptions. If you are providing your own customer service, you have to be available every single day, always, to handle support tickets. If you're only in one timezone, this is not too difficult, but as you expand into new territories, you'll have to add some capability here. At Bobsled Marketing we conduct daily reviews of each client account in each market — responding to customer questions, seller feedback, and reviews, checking inventory levels and performance metrics, and monitoring listings for rogue sellers. Since we have a defined system in place, we're able to repeat this process dozens of times a day and in multiple languages. If your brand is handling its own account, you'll need to create and implement the same kind of repeatable process every day, 365 days a year.

Now, I mentioned that there are programs that Amazon runs for sellers who have consistently provided very high levels of customer service. One of these is Seller

Fulfilled Prime (covered in Chapter 11) — instead of having to send inventory to Amazon's fulfillment centers to be eligible for Prime, you can actually fulfill those orders yourself from your own warehouse. To be eligible for this program, you have to go through a trial, fulfill 300 orders perfectly in a 90-day timeframe, and your seller metrics will also be assessed: whether you have fulfilled orders on time, whether you are responding to customers in a timely fashion and so on. For some businesses, this makes fulfillment for Prime orders more cost effective, since they don't have to pay additional shipping costs to get their inventory to Amazon. It is a more expensive option for many businesses (because they have to fulfill two-day shipping to customers, which is very expensive through third party carriers like UPS and Fedex), but it does allow for more control over inventory, since the merchant holds all inventory themselves rather than splitting it up with Amazon. The company can also choose the locations where they offer SFP, using shipping templates, so they don't have to offer the service in areas where it's unprofitable.

Managing Customer Expectations

Being such a customer-centric platform, many of the people who buy from you will expect every interaction to be positive. Customers have been trained to expect very high levels of service from Amazon, so you have to be ready to meet that expectation at all times.

In the event that you are fulfilling orders yourself, you used to be able to set whatever seller policy you wanted. For example, your terms could state that customers were responsible for the cost of return if they didn't like an item, rather than following Amazon's blanket offer of free returns. This has recently changed, though — third party sales are now immediately covered with free returns. Sellers can, however, charge a re-stocking fee. Of course, customers who have to wear that cost are likely to be very annoyed, because they don't expect it and rarely check seller's individual policies. They won't see a difference between Amazon fulfilling orders and individual sellers fulfilling orders, and so they expect the same level of service and treatment from everyone.

Should they make a complaint to Amazon about something like this, that can compromise your seller metrics as well.

Generally speaking, it's wise to have generous policies when you're selling on Amazon. Give customers the benefit of the doubt, and make it easy for them to love you and leave you glowing reviews. Sure, you might save a few dollars on each returned unit and reduce your return rate over time if you put the responsibility on the customer, but at what cost? What happens when you get hit with a really nasty review that you can't remove? Or what if the customer files an A-to-Z complaint claim, which will really affect your Buy Box performance? Instead of losing those couple of dollars, you can lose large numbers of sales, or even lose your listing. I really recommend not trying to skimp on customer care on Amazon — the upside of taking great care of them is absolutely worth it.

A-to-Z Claims

Amazon guarantees purchases from third-party sellers when a customer buys anything on the platform. The condition of the item purchased and its timely delivery is covered by the Amazon A-to-Z guarantee. For example, if you list a product as new and the customer thinks it's used when they receive it, they can file a claim under the A-to-Z guarantee, and the same if it doesn't arrive within the estimated delivery timeframe. If a customer has waited more than two business days for a response from you, or if the item is defective, they can also make a claim.

If the customer claims any of those things, Amazon will intervene. They will let you know that you have an A-to-Z claim against you, and you have to address it straight away. They become the mediator between you and the customer, and will require you to provide redress to the customer immediately — basically, they'll push you to give the customer whatever they ask for. Having an A-to-Z claim opened against you can significantly affect your seller rating. Should you find yourself in this situation, it will serve you to be hyper-responsive and completely cooperative, as dragging your feet will affect your selling rating and sales metrics even further.

Some sellers find this difficult to swallow. It's costly, and can be frustrating when you're working so hard to provide great service to have to pony up like this. As I've mentioned, Amazon is a high-risk, high-reward platform, and this is one of the costs of doing business there. It's a high-visibility platform that introduces you to whole new market segments, and you just have to pay for the privilege of using it.

Key Operational Aspects

Inventory management is one of the most critical aspects of running any Amazon store, but it becomes even more important when you're expanding into multiple territories. It's very important that you're aware of how quickly your store turns inventory, so that you can send enough inventory to Amazon's fulfillment centers in a timely way to prevent potential stock-outs. During the holidays, this becomes even more important. Amazon takes much longer to receive inventory around the holiday season, because *all* their sellers are trying to get more stock in to meet the increased demand. With 400 million products listed on the platform, you can imagine the mammoth logistical undertaking they have on their hands at every fulfillment center. They have a lot of deliveries that have to be scheduled and processed, and millions of products that need to be scanned and stored, so your delivery can take much longer to be processed. Your freight carriers are also under pressure — they make a much higher volume of deliveries at this time of year, and so your delivery has to be scheduled to fit with both their demands and Amazon's.

As I mentioned earlier, for inventory to be delivered to an Amazon fulfillment center, the freight company has to book an appointment, and stick to it. If the driver misses the window by more than 30 minutes, they will be turned around and told to make another appointment. That would be fine if they could just schedule for the same afternoon, but often the next available appointment is two or three *weeks* away. Then your inventory just sits on a truck somewhere, not moving, while you're running out of inventory and carrying the cost of that shipment. Of course, this is only relevant to sellers sending in inventory via LTL or FTL — if you're using UPS small parcel delivery, the turnaround time for deliveries will be much faster and there are less logistical steps involved because UPS handles it all. Regardless of how you get your inventory in, it's critical to be on top of this if you want your store to be a real success.

If you run out of inventory during the holiday season, it won't affect your seller rating, but it will affect your products' Best Seller Rankings. This is the relative rank of your product in its category. Your rank will go up in number (which is bad — you want to be as close to number one as possible), because you're selling less per day, relative to competitive sellers selling similar products. When you're eventually back in stock, your Best Seller Rank may bounce back quickly if you've only been out of stock for a few days and you have a popular product.

However, it *can* have more of a long term effect. You've lost your rank, which is important, because it determines how your product shows up in the search results. If they have a better (lower) rank, your competitors selling similar products will likely get more sales as their products will potentially show up higher in the search results for relevant searches by customers.

How to Manage Your Inventory

Inventory management is a complex area. It depends very much on demand, and has a seasonal aspect that can further complicate things. To help you handle all the moving pieces of international inventory management, there are a few tools you can use.

First, Amazon has a predictive algorithm that measures your performance and can help you project what demand is going to look like over time. It sits in your Seller Central dashboard, and Amazon can tell you about the unit sales per product over the last 30 days, and based on your current levels of inventory, when they predict you will run out. I've found that this is about 75% accurate — occasionally the inventory count is inaccurate, which in turn messes up the projections. This tool will give you an idea of when you need to send inventory of a particular SKU, but you should definitely go back and double check that the number of available inventory showing in your dashboard matches up with your shipment and sales records for the same time period. At this point in time, the predictive algorithm does not take into account incoming inventory. If you've already sent in a shipment of a particular SKU, it will not be shown in your dashboard — you'll just see that you only have, say, five units left of a particular SKU, even though you have 200 about to arrive. You need to keep a very clear record of what you've sent in and how many sales you've made to stay ahead of this hole in the system.

You need to have a system running to keep an eye on the inventory of every marketplace if you are selling in multiple Amazon territories. It gets even more complex because you're factoring in international freight timelines, so you also must have even more robust prediction capabilities.

It's a duplicated effort across each marketplace to keep this running smoothly. For accounts that we manage across multiple territories, we'll get an indication from the client on the expected lead time with their freight, then back-calculate the requirements for each market. It's the same process in each market, but it comes down to understanding the demand and time considerations at play in each one. If you're going to be managing your Amazon marketplaces in-house, there are some software solutions out there which will help manage this element for you — one good example is www.forecast.ly. There is new software coming out all the time to help you optimize your Amazon performance, and so I've listed all my current recommendations on the Book Resource page on the Bobsled Marketing website — bobsledmarketing.com/amazon-expansion-plan-resources. These are the options we've seen performing with the highest level of accuracy and that may be a better fit for you than the native Amazon algorithm, particularly as you expand and have more inventory streams to manage.

Finally, you need to make a decision about how you barcode your products. As we discussed earlier, Amazon requires every item that is processed through their fulfillment centers to have an Amazon FNSKU barcode applied to it. This makes the item discoverable by their packing robots and fulfillment staff, and you or your manufacturer can apply these labels prior to sending them your inventory, or have Amazon apply the labels when they receive the shipment.

Amazon charges 20 cents per unit to apply the barcodes for you. If you have a very large shipment, that can be a costly process, and occasionally, the wrong barcode ends up on your inventory. This is particularly likely to happen during high-volume times (such as during the holidays). If it happens that they incorrectly sticker your units, then your customers get the wrong products. Your customers complain, and after a certain number of complaints, Amazon will decide that your product is not accurately described, and they will pull that product listing from the platform… because of a mistake that they made. If the problem is widespread enough, they may even look at banning your entire account. Where possible — especially around the holidays — arrange to have the FNSKU barcodes applied before the inventory is sent to Amazon. You can generate the barcodes yourself in Seller Central, download them as a PDF and print them as stickers to be applied to each unit.

How to Manage Returns From International Markets

Within your 'home' market, the customer simply ships the return item back to your facility, where you can test and repackage the items as is appropriate, but this process is more challenging when you're selling in markets where you don't have a physical presence. Amazon won't return inventory to you if you don't have a physical mailing address in that country. For example, if a customer returns your product, and the product is not in a condition that Amazon can resell it in, Amazon will keep charging you warehouse fees until you arrange a solution. You can't just send the items straight back to your facility, either.

One solution is to engage the services of a repackaging provider (often part of a 3PL company). They will find out from you what needs to be in each package (instructions, parts and so on), then they will test that the unit is functional and in good condition, and then repackage it in packaging that you have provided to them. This is particularly useful if you have a high-value item that would be costly for you to dispose of. Alternately, if the item is not in resale condition or is a lower price-point, you can elect to have Amazon dispose of it for you. Finally, you can send it to a forwarding facility and have them ship it back to you, but this really only makes sense when you have a high-value, lightweight product with a justifiable quantity of units to be returned.

Chapter Six: Marketing Your Amazon Store

Just because you now have your Amazon account set up, it does not mean that you'll automatically have huges sales consistently rolling in. Remember — it's not a set and forget platform. As with any sales channel, Amazon will perform best for your business if you approach it with a clear marketing strategy that will help increase profitability over time.

In this chapter, we're going to explore some of the marketing tactics you can use to ensure that your products get as much visibility and traction as possible, and that you are converting as much of the resulting traffic as you possibly can.

Search Algorithm:

The first thing to understand about marketing on Amazon is that there are three elements in the search algorithm that contribute to your products' performance: relevance, sales velocity, and conversion rate.

Relevance

The first of these is relevance. For example, if a customer searches for 'white chalk paint' and you have a product that *is* white chalk paint and those words are listed in your title, then your product will show up as having high relevance to that query — much more than if you had just 'white paint' or 'paint' in your title. This is where your keyword research is really important. Having the right keywords in your title, bullet points and metadata is one of the best ways to increase your relevance.

Listing your product in the right category is also important for increasing your relevance — some buyers are attracted to selling in a less competitive category, because they could (in theory) rank higher in that category relative to a very competitive category. The downside is that if you list a product in a category that doesn't make any logical sense, that can be detrimental when you set up PPC campaigns and can undo the lift you would get from just choosing the right category.

The keywords that perform well in PPC campaigns are a really rich source of insight into what's driving traffic to your listings, and we'll talk more about PPC campaigns later in this chapter. In your PPC search term reports, you'll be able to see with much more clarity which terms are punching above their weight. A good indicator is when there's not as much search volume for a particular term, and you're winning every sale for that term, because you're the only one bidding on that keyword. Then it might be useful for you to integrate that keyword back into your listing so that you also show up for it in organic results.

Generally speaking, keywords on Amazon are going to be the same as what you will find on Google. Consumers will often use Google and Amazon for the same purpose — finding products, price comparisons and so on — so some sellers just use the tools available for Google keyword research for their Amazon keywords as well. There *are* plenty of Amazon-specific keyword research tools, but again, your PPC campaigns tend to be the ultimate keyword harvest ground, because you can see exactly which terms are producing the best results. Another interesting strategy is misspelled keywords. A lot of sellers are not thinking about how their brand name or product name could be misspelled, and so you have an opportunity to target phonetic spellings of your keywords, as well as international spellings (such as British English instead of American English).

Sales velocity

Sales velocity is the number of sales your product has had in a specific timeframe, relative to your competitors. If Product A has sold 10 units per day for a month, and Product B has sold 100 units per day for a month, then all other things being equal, Product B would rank higher thanks to its greater sales velocity.

Best Seller Rank is the algorithm Amazon uses to index the popularity of products across categories. It's a relative ranking system that shows how many products have been purchased recently. A Best Seller Rank of #1 means that you have the bestselling product in that whole category, a Best Seller Rank of #20,000 means, obviously, that you're the 20,000th bestseller in that category (and #20,000 can actually be a reasonable position in a competitive category, given that there are over 400 million products on Amazon).

You can increase your sales velocity effectively with Lightning Deals (four-hour deals that Amazon runs periodically). If, during an a four-hour period, you get over a thousand sales, your Best Seller Rank is going to improve drastically. This creates a virtuous cycle, as people will see your product higher in the search results than they would have previously, and will be more likely to keep buying it at full price. This will eventually peter off, but the increase in visibility for that timeframe can create its own momentum.

Another option to increase your sales rank is through PPC campaigns. If you're running effective campaigns that result in sales, then that will help your sales rank as well. It will help your organic rank, because you're getting more sales overall, and it will also help your organic rank for the keyword you got the PPC sales from. For example, if someone searches for 'white chalk paint' and they see your ad, click it and buy the product through that trail, Amazon captures the keywords that were used (organically or paid) so your relative ranking for that keyword will increase as well. PPC can help your organic sales rank overall, and for specific keywords you're trying to rank for.

Conversion rate

Finally, your conversion rate also factors into product search rankings. This is the number of people who actually bought the product relative to the total number of people who looked at the product page.

The thing to understand with conversion rates is that a good conversion percentage for one product may be completely unattainable for another type of product. For example, one of our clients is in the beauty category with a great product, and has a conversion rate of about 20%. That would be inconceivable in the women's' jeans category. The total value of the conversion rate is relative, but there isn't any way to see what your competitor's conversion rate is in order to benchmark your product against others like it. You can only track your own conversion rate over time and try to optimize it.

The way your conversion rate is calculated is: *Sales / total traffic = conversion rate.*

In order to optimize your conversion rate, then, you need to increase the proportion of sales relative to your total traffic. This is why getting your PPC campaigns right is so important — you want to be sending highly qualified traffic to your page so that you get more sales, rather than getting more traffic that bounces off the page and skews the conversion rate in the wrong direction. The other factor is on-page optimization — great product images, great copy, and great product reviews. You want each of the elements that you can control to be working hard to win that sale. Make your product listing as appealing as possible to the most carefully targeted group of people you can find.

You can think of these three elements under a single idea: you want to make Amazon as much money as possible, in as few clicks as possible. Space on Amazon's platform is precious real estate. They don't want people to be clicking around a lot — they want customers to find what they need, and then purchase it as soon as possible. If your products are relevant, they've been proven to sell well in the past, and have been proven to be compelling enough for good conversion rates, then that's a winner in Amazon's eyes, and they'll rank you higher in the search results than they will for someone else whose product doesn't tick all three boxes as well.

Product Listing Copy

This is one of the most critical aspects of creating a high-ranking, high-converting product listing. First, you need to identify the important keywords for your products. Google Keyword Planner and other Amazon-specific keyword research tools are the best options for doing this research. Ideally, you are looking for underutilized, high-volume keywords. Then you need to go into the meta-data in the back end of your product listing, to the keywords section. There, you can add your selected keywords. A lot of people skip this, but it can create a really easy, quick win for the visibility of your product in the search results.

You should also list the most important keywords in the title of your product listing, based on what you have found in your keyword research and what you know customers have searched for in the past. You also need to make sure that the title makes sense to a human, and is not so stuffed full of keywords that it would only appeal to an algorithm.

Because Amazon doesn't share the details of how their algorithms work, we don't know for sure whether including keywords in your bullet points and product descriptions is effective or not. Personally, at the time of writing, I had not seen anything that would compel an argument either way. Since that's the case, I'd recommend taking the middle ground with keywords throughout the rest of your listing — it can't hurt to have them included, but don't overdo it or stuff the page.

Think about your own experience using Amazon. When you look at search results on Amazon, you see a thumbnail image of the product, the title, and the price. Those three elements have to be compelling, and they have to communicate the key message about the product in order to get a customer's attention.

(Three important things to note here: firstly, having a higher price point than competing sellers doesn't mean a listing will perform worse — if someone is looking for a premium item, they might actually be put off by a lower price point. Secondly, the title, image and price details also have to be compliant with Amazon's display rules — the main product image has to be on a white background, there can't be any props and so on. Finally, another factor here is to see how your product page shows up in mobile search, and whether the product title and other elements are truncated because they're too long, as this can compromise conversions on mobile).

Then when you get through to the product page, you see the primary product image, the secondary product images, and then the bullet points (we'll cover some best practices for product images shortly). The bullet points are where you expect to see the most compelling features and benefits of the product — all the smaller details should be addressed in the product description.

When you're thinking about how to structure the information about your product, take a look at the information hierarchy Amazon has built into the product pages. The most important information all shows above the fold: the visual content, the headline that gets the attention of the right customers, and the easily-digested bullet points that let the reader know if this product could be the right option for them. This follows the basic rules of sales copywriting: you want to get their attention, pique their interest, stimulate their desire for the product and then invite them to act.

Product Imagery Best Practices

Amazon has very specific rules about how sellers can behave on their platform, and how you present your product photos is no exception. They're quite strict about this, so even if you see other sellers bending the rules, I do not recommend doing it yourself. There are varying degrees of consequences — from a message from Amazon giving you a slap on the wrist and telling you to change something, to instantly having your account shut down and being banned from ever opening one again.

(Bannable offences include paying people for reviews, buying your own products to bump your metrics, or anything to do with manipulating the sales of your products, selling inauthentic products, or being aggressive with customers.)

To make sure your products are represented in the best possible way (and in a way that doesn't draw the attention of Amazon's audit robots), here are some best practices to follow for each of the 7 - 9 image slots that Amazon provides for each product listing.

- The lead product photo must be on a white background, showing only the product — no props, packaging or background imagery.

- The product should be shown with packaging, either displayed inside the packaging or right next to it to show the customer what to expect when it arrives.

- Where appropriate, the product should be shown in use. You should show it being used as intended (by a model when it makes sense), staged in an ideal setting.

- Include a lifestyle photo where appropriate. This should show how the product solves the customer's problem as they put it into use in their life.

- 'Feature and benefit' image: use a text overlay on the image that points out the different features of the product, and how each of them benefits the customer.

- Product photo with 'badges' displaying additional benefits that help consumers to make a purchase decision. These can include safety and quality assurances, product awards, media features, etc.

- Other image options include dimensional images (when a core benefit of a product is its size, an image that puts the product in proportion can be helpful), before and after images (to demonstrate the effectiveness of the product), or digital product elements (for example, if a mobile app accompanies the product, it's useful to highlight the functions of the app through a sequence of screenshots. Ideally the screenshots would also be annotated with features or benefits).

- Finally, *all* images should have very high resolution — a minimum of 1,000 px is an absolute must.

We are also commonly asked about how to add video to your Amazon listing. This is only possible if you're on the Vendor program, which also allows you to have more images for each listing, along with comparison tables and other visual elements not available on the FBA program.

Product Reviews

Product reviews are really important for establishing credibility and social proof on Amazon. There was an interesting study from Northwestern University that showed that most shoppers trust reviews that rate the product and seller between 4 and 4.5 stars *more* than they trust 5-star ratings. Having a few middle-range reviews of your products help to make your overall rating seem more credible to skeptical buyers. Across 40 categories tested, sales increased along with the star rating up to 4.5 stars, but after 4.5 stars sales actually dropped off. A product with all 5-star ratings just looks too good to be true and makes people skeptical.

A few other key findings from the research that are pertinent for brands selling on Amazon:

- Negative reviews help make buying decisions. The company PowerReviews, who provided data for the Northwestern University study, also cites that 82% of shoppers specifically seek out negative product reviews.

- Reviews matter less for cheap products. Star ratings had a stronger influence on expensive items compared to the inexpensive items within the same category.

- The ideal number of reviews varies. When reviews are shorter, more reviews matter. If reviews are lengthier, the number of reviews has a less significant impact.

That said, Amazon's product review ecosystem is a critical part of their proposition. It's estimated that 61% of consumers read online reviews before making a purchase decision, and reviews from real customers provide social proof and a sense of reduced risk around the product they're researching. Sadly, less than 5% of Amazon customers actually end up writing a review for products that they buy.

For brands on Amazon, this creates a paradox: your product has no reviews, so it gets no sales. And because you get no sales, you get no reviews. It's critical to break this vicious catch-22 cycle and begin to build up genuine reviews for your product assortment on Amazon. The good news is that you don't need all 5-star reviews, and there are a few ways to start building up your products credibility with reviews. Let's walk through a few of the common methods of getting reviews, the step-by-step process we use instead at Bobsled Marketing, and cardinal rules to prevent disaster with your account.

Before getting into the weeds, it's important to note that Amazon is constantly updating the rules and requirements for how brands operate on its platform, particularly around reviews.

Prior to October 2016, Amazon did allow brands to provide free or discounted product samples to customers in exchange for a review. This was a popular and effective way to generate product reviews, fast.

Amazon recognized that product listings which were padded with reviews from customers who all got a product for free do not inspire consumer confidence. There was an eventual backlash in the media against brands who are seen to be excessively boosting their product review numbers through such promotions. The website *Fakespot* allows users to see what percentage of reviews on a product appear to be "fake" and boycott those brands.

So in October 2016, "incentivized reviews" were banned, meaning that brands can no longer *require* a customer to write a review in exchange for a free or discounted product.

It really pays to be closely attuned to Amazon's rules and keep up to date to prevent product or account suspension or even being banned from Amazon for not following the rules. It's extremely important that you recognize that the folks at Amazon are no fools. They know that sellers will game the system if they can, and that this compromises customer trust. I strongly recommend against trying to game it or 'get one over' Amazon — you won't, and it will just damage your long-term position on the platform.

That said, it is important to have a baseline of reviews. Products without any reviews are less compelling and customers don't want to take the risk on you. To get around this problem, there are five ways I recommend that you get real, high-quality reviews.

<u>Method #1: The Amazon Vine Program</u>

Amazon has its own program for capturing quality, genuine reviews from their top reviewers, called the Vine Program. The Vine program is only available to Vendors (that is, brands selling via Vendor Express or Vendor Central), and Amazon takes care of all the logistics. The catch is that it's a paid program. It can cost a couple thousand dollars to have Amazon run a Vine Review campaign, and of course you need to provide the products to reviewers for free. The program is also not particularly scalable. Amazon limits how many units can be shipped (typically 15 - 100 depending on the category). So brands may only be able to generate a few reviews per product with the Vine program.

The benefit is that you get excellent quality reviews (reviewers are selected by Amazon based on prior quality of reviews and number of reviews written), all within Amazon's terms of service, and all the logistics of selecting reviewers and sending samples are taken care of for you.

Method #2: Post-Purchase Email Follow-Up

It's possible to boost the average product review rate by a few percentage points by sending customers a reminder after their purchase through the Amazon messaging system. This option is available to brands selling on the Seller Central platform.

You don't want to annoy customers with too many post-purchase emails — Amazon themselves send post-purchase emails to customers, so you'll want to be short and sweet, and provide the customer with value first, and then a good reason for writing the review. Appeal to the natural human desire to be helpful, support a small business, or perhaps crack a joke or two if that's consistent with your brand. Other successes we've seen with post-purchase email follow-ups is to add value to the customer by providing helpful tips on how to use the product or a free ebook which is relevant to the product.

You can execute this strategy manually through the Amazon messaging system, or through third party software tools like Salesbacker or Feedback Genius. Software tools allow you to create a sequence of emails.

It's important to know that customers are able to opt out of receiving messages from Sellers, and you don't want to annoy a buyer with too many emails or irrelevant messages. Add value and be sparing in your follow-up emails, and you can increase the odds of more reviews – but not guarantee it.

Method #3: Leverage Your List

If your brand has a pre-existing email subscriber database or active followers on social media, this can be a great tool to quickly establish more sales and reviews for your products.

Currently, Amazon *does* allow customers to post reviews for products which were not ordered through their own customer account. This means that if you have existing customers who are willing to write a product review for items they bought through your online store or elsewhere, this can quickly give you a leg-up. This could be done through an email newsletter or social media campaign which describes how important product reviews are to the success of your brand on Amazon. Your most loyal customers will often be willing to lend a helping hand to a brand that they've had a great experience with.

The downside is that the reviews will not show up as a "Verified purchase", which lacks the credibility of a verified purchase made through Amazon. Still, these are better than no reviews at all.

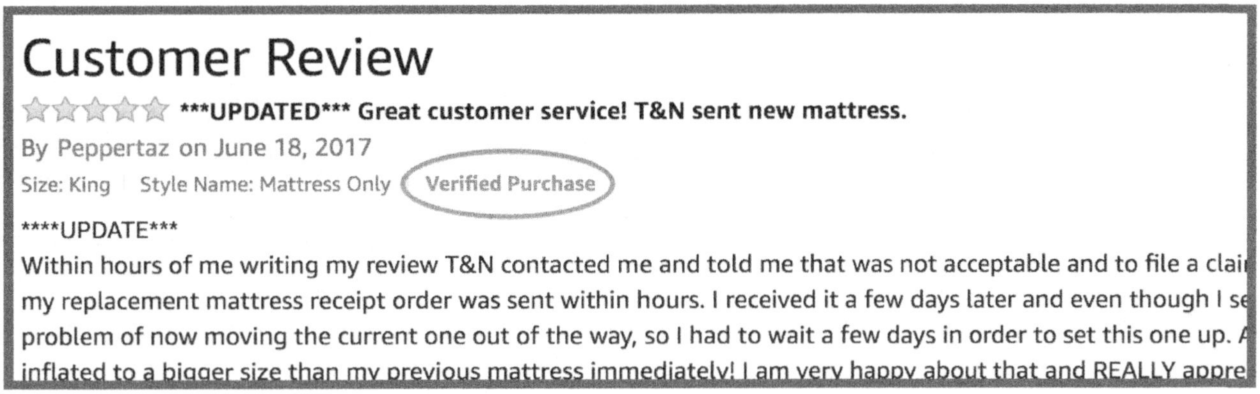

Customer Review

UPDATED Great customer service! T&N sent new mattress.

By Peppertaz on June 18, 2017

Size: King | Style Name: Mattress Only | Verified Purchase

****UPDATE***

Within hours of me writing my review T&N contacted me and told me that was not acceptable and to file a clai
my replacement mattress receipt order was sent within hours. I received it a few days later and even though I se
problem of now moving the current one out of the way, so I had to wait a few days in order to set this one up. A
inflated to a bigger size than my previous mattress immediately! I am very happy about that and REALLY appre

This strategy can be used by both Sellers and Vendors.

If I didn't belabor the point enough already, please don't be tempted to write your own reviews, or even have colleagues, friends or family do this for you. It's not worth the risk!

Method 4: Follow Up On Seller Feedback

Many customers (and Sellers!) do not understand the difference between Product Reviews and Seller Feedback. Seller Feedback only shows on the Seller detail page, which few customers check. Product Reviews show on the product listing page. Frustratingly, Amazon does not make it particularly clear to customers what the difference is. So when customers submit positive Seller Feedback (which is different from Product Reviews), it's worthwhile to ask them to copy and paste the feedback into a product review as well - explaining that doing so will allow other customers to see their helpful feedback.

This method could be the simplest, fastest and most effective method of them all. It works best if you can jump immediately on positive Seller Feedback while the customer still has that warm, happy feeling about your product - another great reason to be monitoring your Seller account daily.

Method 5: Packaging slips

Brands have an opportunity to include product, customer service, or warranty information as a packaging slip. This collateral can be well designed and compelling enough to make the customer take an action like writing a product review.

It can be cumbersome for a customer to manually type in a long URL to leave a product review, so a great idea to increase your likelihood of a review is to include a QR code which can be scanned instead.

When designing packaging slips, be careful to ensure that they are compliant with Amazon's Terms of Service. Your packaging and included collateral shouldn't explicitly divert customers away from Amazon.

Cardinal Rules of Reviews

Before we wrap up this section, I want to share a couple of cardinal rules with you. These are *extremely* important but something that Amazon sellers might assume are okay if they don't know otherwise.

1. Never, ever review your own product on Amazon.

This is explicitly against Amazon's Terms of Service and definitely not worth the pain of having your product listing (or even entire Seller account!) shut down. In fact it's wise to not have anyone from the same IP address (e.g. your home or office where you might be using Amazon) review your products.

2. Never, ever offer an incentive for a positive review.
This includes cash bonus, a discount on future sales, entry into a contest... Again, any potential benefit in the number of reviews is not worth your account being shut down.

3. Don't play with fire.
At the end of the day, product reviews can make a huge difference in sales. Getting a baseline of genuine product reviews is a critical component of our own Amazon Launch and Optimization process. But doing it properly, within Amazon's Terms of Service and in a way that customers will see as genuine, is the most important thing to keep in mind.

Other Traffic Sources

You can send traffic to your Amazon listing from off-platform sources as well. Facebook and other social media platforms can be good sources of lifting your traffic, as well as PPC campaigns on external search engines, joint ventures and so on. Some Amazon experts are of the view that Amazon *weights* traffic, meaning that traffic that goes to your page from within the Amazon ecosystem has less of an impact on your search ranking than traffic from external sources, but we really don't know. I think you should hedge your bets and bring as much traffic to your listings as you can, from whatever sources are available to you.

Running Facebook or Google PPC ad campaigns can have a very tangible effect on your Amazon traffic and performance. We're seeing a pattern emerge with a few Bobsled clients around this — they run Facebook ads to their own ecommerce store, which creates a surge in interest in their products. Potential customers visit their store, like the look of the products, and then open Amazon in a new tab and buy the product *there*, either because they can get it delivered on Prime or because they feel more comfortable purchasing from a new brand via Amazon.

Typically those campaigns run at a loss initially (the ROI happens once the customer makes a second purchase), but there are two upsides: customers who purchase through the ecommerce store are added to an email list where they can be remarketed to; and the Amazon listing sees an increase in performance *without* any additional ad spend or attention.

The other option is to run PPC ads on external platforms directly to your Amazon listing. This works particularly well if your product is available on Prime, because you can get a very short feedback loop on what is appealing to your market. Some sellers are (understandably) concerned that if they send a lot of traffic to their Amazon listings and this traffic doesn't convert, it will hurt their conversion rates and search ranking. As a result, sellers are very hesitant to try this option, but as you'll see, it's generally not something to be particularly concerned about.

What is clear is that people trust recommendations from peers and influencers, and a positive review from a blogger or influencer on social media may help convince a customer to buy a product even if there are few or no existing product reviews.

PPC Examples

As I mentioned, there are a couple of different approaches you can take to running PPC to your ecommerce presence — either sending traffic directly to your own ecommerce store and none to Amazon, or sending traffic to your Amazon listing instead. We'll explore both methods here with some examples from Bobsled clients.

Client One:

- This client started running Facebook Ads to promote a specific product on their Shopify site. They were not running any traffic whatsoever to their Amazon store.

- With an average customer acquisition cost of $30 to acquire a $45 average sale, they were getting great results up front (as it's not unusual in ecommerce to break even or have a loss on the first sale if customer lifetime value makes it worthwhile).

- We saw a significant increase in sales on Amazon for the product set over the past two months as a result of this campaign, even though no traffic was being directed there through the ads: customers were seeing the ad on Facebook, going to the ecommerce store to do some initial research, then checking to see if the same products were available to buy on Amazon and buying there.

Client Two:

- This client also started a PPC campaign, but decided to send their traffic directly to Amazon.

- This client was attracted to the low-touch FBA model, as having Amazon fulfill retail orders was better and more efficient than doing it themselves. They continued this approach with their advertising and saw significant increases in their Amazon sales.

- They were initially concerned that sending more traffic from outside the platform would negatively impact their conversion rates. While this is a risk, highly-targeted traffic from people who are interested enough to click on an ad impacted their conversion rates in a positive way.

Some experts who don't believe the 'weighted traffic' theory think that traffic outside Amazon helps Amazon to recognize the product's popularity outside the platform and could help to boost results. This is the case for other marketing efforts like PR, influencer outreach and more.

Influencer Marketing

Many brands are familiar with working with bloggers and social media influencers in order to get more exposure to relevant customers. You can use this same strategy of working with online influencers to promote your products on Amazon.

Online influencers work with brands to promote their products as a means of monetizing their blog or social media presence, and influencers with the most reach often command a significant upfront fee. But as an Amazon seller, you may be able to sweeten the deal with no additional cost to you by leveraging the Amazon Associates program.

Amazon Associates was one of the first online "affiliate marketing" programs, and allows online influencers to receive a commission on purchases made on Amazon when a follower uses their personal affiliate link. Amazon describes it the following way: "When website owners and bloggers who are Associates create links and customers click through those links and buy products from Amazon, they earn referral fees… Provide customers the convenience of referring them to a trusted site where they can immediately purchase the products you advertise on your site. And when they do, you can earn up to 10% in referral fees".

Amazon does not charge Sellers separately for this perk, it is covered in the separate selling costs and fees that Sellers pay to Amazon.

Here's how a partnership with an online influencer could work.

1. Identify a list of bloggers and social media influencers who are active in your category and have an active and relevant audience. Some influencers who have a broader reach might charge you anywhere from a couple hundred to a couple thousand dollars upfront for a blog review or social media post. This would be in

addition to the trailing commission that they'd get from the Amazon Associates program. However, some influencers who are just starting out might be happy to negotiate a smaller upfront fee or even waive their fee, knowing that they'll receive an ongoing commission on sales.

2. Optional - provide the blogger with an exclusive discount that their readers or followers can use to buy your products on Amazon, for example a 20% off discount which is available for 2 weeks.

3. Provide the blogger with free sample(s) either by shipping product directly of through Amazon's Multi-Channel Fulfillment option.

4. The influencer creates content which promotes your products to their followers, and your product listings get an influx of relevant traffic which is more likely to convert. Followed by an effective post-purchase email sequence, you can leverage the influx of sales to pick up genuine product reviews.

Influencer marketing can also help with getting product reviews. Strong backlinks to your product pages from credible sources, including blogs and articles, will help drive traffic to your product pages.

Chapter Seven: Advertising on Amazon

Brands and retailers are shifting major advertising budgets to the Amazon platform at the expense of incumbents like Google and Facebook. This is because Amazon is turning out to be an increasingly effective marketing channel. Relative to other advertising channels, brands can reach customers at a low cost, the path to purchase is very short, and it's where 59% of consumers start their product searches.

A question that new brands often ask is, "how do I get my products to appear at the top of search results on Amazon?" As you've seen from the earlier chapters, it's impossible to guarantee such a result from any SEO or organic marketing strategy. The good news is that advertising does allow you to rank at the top for any keyword you're interested in – for a price. If you know the outcome that you want, whether that be ranking for a strategic keyword, knocking your competitor out, build awareness and sales for your brand and products, or simply driving more sales with a predictable cost of acquisition, advertising is a powerful tool.

There are two broad types of advertising that are native to Amazon: Pay Per Click advertising (PPC) and display or programmatic advertising through the Amazon Advertising Platform (AAP).

At Bobsled Marketing, we offer both services. Pay Per Click advertising (PPC) management is a standalone service that we offer, as well as being a cornerstone component of all our Amazon Channel Management services. This is because PPC provides a very measurable form of acquiring sales on Amazon: ad spend can be closely monitored, with a clear ROI. You can see exactly how much it costs to acquire a sale, and vary your budget accordingly.

Advertising with AAP, which is part of the Amazon Media Group (AMG – Amazon loves their acronyms!) is more focused on building brand and product awareness than driving immediate sales. It has less of a direct ROI than PPC advertising, which always links back to product sales. AAP is generally most suitable for very large brands who are already buying media through advertising agencies. This is because many smaller companies don't have dedicated brand marketing budgets, and the minimum spend is pretty steep. Depending on whether you're working directly with Amazon or through an agency, you may need to commit $15,000 or more in monthly advertising spend.

Types of PPC placements on Amazon

There are three types of PPC campaigns on Amazon: Sponsored Products, Headline Search, and Product Display (available to Vendors using AMS only).

1. **Sponsored products ads** are keyword targeted cost per click search ads that appear below the search results, on the right hand side of the search results page AND on product detail pages (the "Sponsored products related to this item" section).

   Sponsored product ads are a great way to get additional sales for brands who are familiar with the benefits of their products, the target audience who would be looking for their products, and the search queries this audience uses. If you manage to get the targeting keywords right, sponsored products can do wonders for sales in a short timeframe.

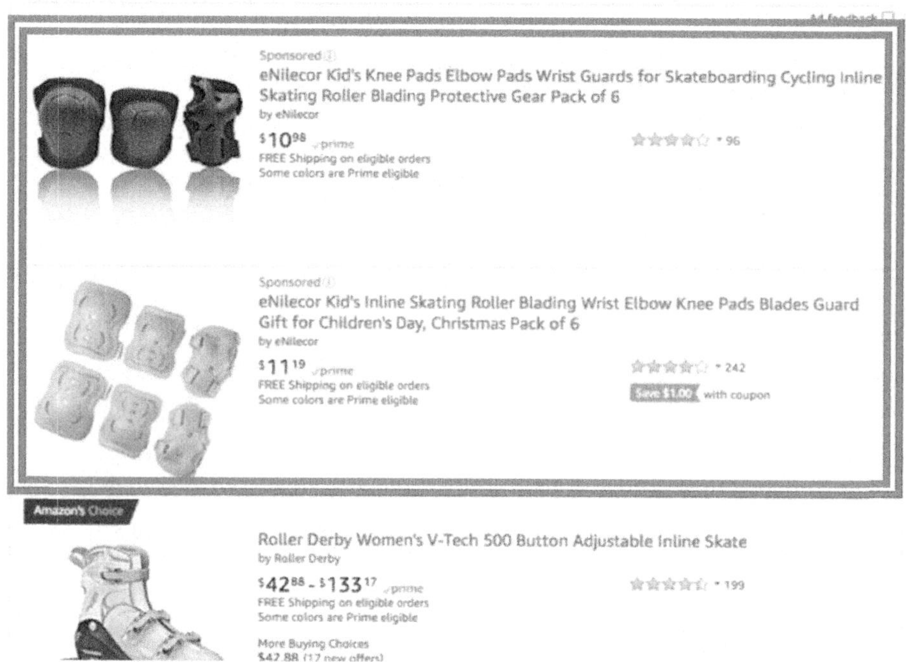

Above: an example of two Sponsored Product ads that sit above the first organic search result for the query 'roller blades'.

2. **Product display ads** are product- or interest-targeted cost per click ads that appear on the related product details page.

   These are the only types of ads which are not targeted by keyword, so they come with some benefits which are unique only to them.

   One scenario where the product display ads would really come in handy is launching a full frontal attack on your competition. Creating different campaigns targeting competitor ASINS and illustrating your products benefit over theirs in the copy.

   You can also run product display ads targeting interests, but we'd only recommend this strategy when your target audience's interests are really specific. (Example: you are selling hiking shoes only and are targeting people who like hiking).

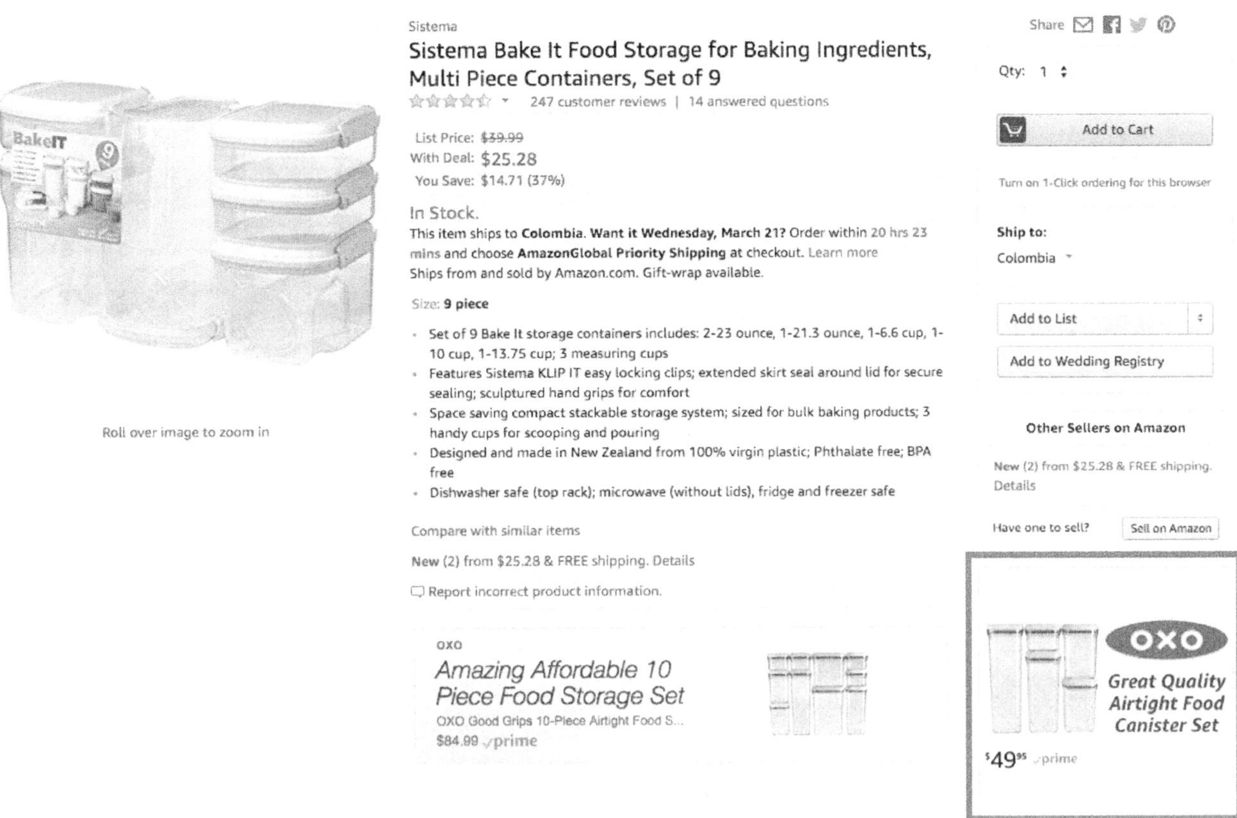

Above: a Product Display Ad where the brand is targeting one of its competitors.

3. **Headline search ads** are (CPC) search ads that are keyword targeted and appear at the top of the first page of search results. These ads are great to increase visibility and interact with the customer at the very beginning of his purchase process, as they appear at the top of the search results.

   Another great scenario to use headline search ads is when you have an assortment of compatible, complementary products, because in the headline search ad you can add up to 3 products.

   Headline search ads offer writing up your own ad title (with several limitations, like using imperatives "the best, No #1, best seller etc.) so you can test different copies of the ad and find the one that converts best.

   They can also be used as a short term solution if your product does not rank well organically (getting some paid 1st page exposure, when you are not ranking well for the free one).

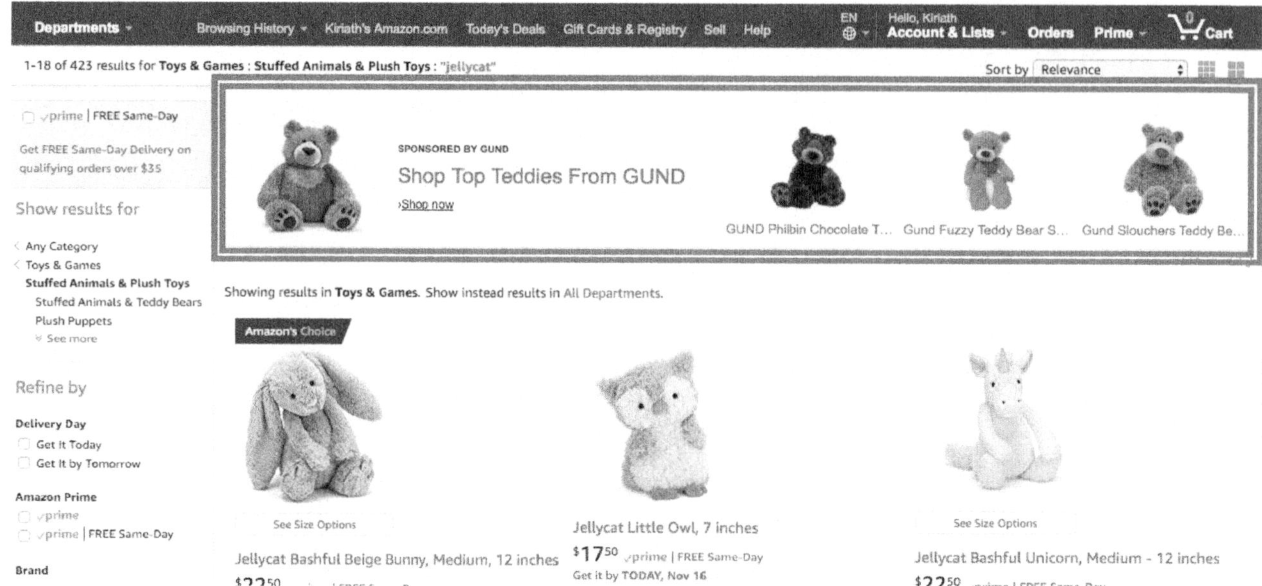

Above: example of a Headline Search Ad where the search query ("Jellycat") resulted in a competitor (Gund) displaying an ad. We call this competitor targeting an 'offense' strategy.

Measuring results from PPC campaigns

Even if you're familiar with PPC on other advertising platforms, Amazon has its own quirks. Here's an overview guide to key metrics that you should be tracking in your campaigns.

- Impressions: the number of times your ads have been shown to shoppers. If your goal with advertising on Amazon is measurable sales, impressions are not a metric that you should be too concerned about in isolation. Amazon's PPC programs do not charge for impressions.
- Clicks: A click occurs when a shopper clicks on your ad, and this is how advertisers are charged. Amazon tracks clicks at the keyword and campaign level.

- Click through rate (CTR). The percentage of shoppers who click on an advertisement, versus those who saw it. This metric informs how relevant the ad is to the search query. A strong click through rate indicates a highly relevant campaign. Less relevant keywords will have lower CTRs and often lower conversions. Generally, we want to see a higher CTR than 0.04%. Otherwise it may indicate that the advertisement that's showing is not enticing enough for shoppers to click on. This could be driven by creative (image, product title), other product information (reviews, price), or relevance of how the ad has been targeted.
- Advertising Cost of Sales (ACoS) is the most common metric for measuring individual campaign performance as well as overall performance of your advertising spend. If you're familiar with Return on Ad Spend (ROAS), it's basically the inverse calculation.
- Average Cost Per Click (ACPC). Average amount spent for a click. Amazon reports on this an aggregate level as well as a keyword basis.
- Detail Page View. Amazon tracks how often a shopper comes back to your page and views the product.
- Spend. You want to know how much you're spending on an aggregate level as well as a keyword basis.
- Units sold. The total number of products sold within 14 days of a user clicking on your ad. This is the key metric for sales attribution. Amazon reports on this metric on a 1, 7, and 14 day basis. At Bobsled, we've found that we have 60-80% of sales attributed within 7 days, with the remaining sales showing up in the following week. 'Jumping the gun' and trying to analyze the success of your campaigns in less than a week is not going to provide accurate insights. A good PPC specialist acts on full and complete data, and that's why it's critical to exercise patience when reviewing your campaigns.

Many brands want to know how clicks are attributed in scenarios where there are multiple sellers, or when a user has clicked on a brand's ads several times. Amazon uses a 'Last Click Attribution' model when deciding which campaign (or advertiser) gets attributed with a sale. This means if a shopper has clicked on multiple ads before buying a product, it's the most recent click before the purchase that gets 'awarded' with the sale. Amazon will not charge you for sales made by shoppers who click on your ad and end up buying a product from another seller. The "Other ASIN" report is where Amazon tells you which product a customer ended up buying after clicking on your ads.

How Amazon compares against other advertising platforms

Google and Facebook track campaigns in real-time, whereas Amazon has the aforementioned latency period of up to 2 weeks. This is because Amazon reflects the way that consumers shop on Amazon – sales often happen after some research or consultation with other household members. In this way, Amazon may seem frustrating to brands who are familiar with Google and Facebook. Assessing campaigns daily or even weekly can be counter-productive. While you'll want to *check* campaigns daily, making decisions to pause or cancel campaigns should be done far less frequently.

In general, Amazon has less sophisticated reporting than the incumbent platforms. Amazon only released a 60-day lookback period to Seller Central users in early 2018. However, Amazon clearly recognizes the great revenue-generating potential of its advertising program, and is releasing new features and reporting constantly.

Anatomy of Advertising campaigns

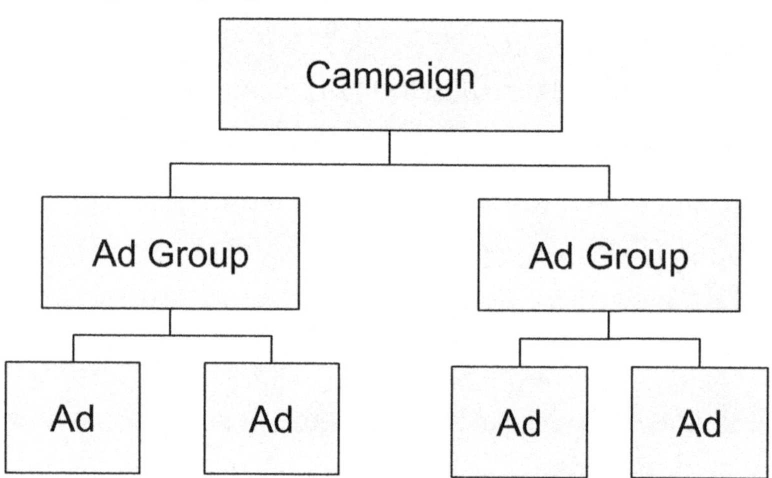

There are two types of advertising campaigns, Manual and Automatic. With Automatic, Amazon chooses the audience to display to, using keywords from the back-end of the listing and the copy in the product type. Manual campaigns are built by the advertiser. We definitely recommend including 1 ASIN per campaign for AMS and SC accounts. Having only 1 ASIN per campaign makes it easier to review results, and easier to scale campaigns once you start adding more ad groups.

Ad groups are available only to Seller Central users. Ad Groups sit under the Campaign. And finally, Ads sit beneath Ad Groups. Note that ads will either show as 'Running' or 'Ineligible' - you can't determine eligibility at the Ad Group or Campaign level.

So when should you pause or cancel a campaign? It depends on the goals for each product in your assortment, and you want to be careful to allow an appropriate amount of time for the data to settle before making rash decisions. But there are some good reasons for pausing or cancelling a campaign.

a) Pausing a campaign if inventory is low and there is an increasing risk of a stock-out.

b) Pausing a campaign until the product gets more reviews, if the conversion rate is poor.

c) Pausing or terminating a campaign because another campaign or campaign type is more profitable. For example, you may choose to terminate a Sponsored Product campaign in favor of a Headline Search campaign that has a better return on ad spend.

d) Pausing or terminating a campaign because of under-performance. Sometimes if a product does not convert, and you've tried everything from the advertising side, the best thing to do is terminate it.

How to get started

If you don't have any PPC (pay-per-click) campaigns running on Amazon yet, you should start by running an automated campaign for two weeks. This is where Amazon will just use the keywords indexed in the back end of your listing, as well as pulling keywords from your title and description, and it will start an automatic campaign based on their best guess about what your keywords mean. What's useful about doing this first is that you don't have to manage the campaigns yourself — while the automated campaign might bid on some dud keywords, they can also turn up strong keywords you hadn't thought of. You get to have a little bit of data around which keywords perform really well and which ones don't perform as well as you thought they would, while working with a low budget while you're just starting out.

Once you have your Automatic campaigns set up, you can start harvesting useful keyword data from the Customer Search Term Reports. These reports are in the Advertising reports section in Seller Central, and are an extremely helpful tool for understanding new search terms that can be used to optimize both the ads as well as the customer-facing product title and copy on the product page. We recommend looking at this report weekly, and identifying search terms which have made a lot of sales in the past week.

Based on the findings from the automatic campaigns and your Customer Search Term Reports, you can start building out manual campaigns. You'll want to think strategically about how to group those campaigns. A lot of the time you might group them by product or product type, or you might create campaigns for specific seasonal events and holidays. Whenever you want to measure something specific, make sure you run a separate campaign to get accurate data. What you don't want to do (unless you want to be spending hours combing through your results and analysing the data), is to create one big campaign with keywords for all of your products. It becomes impossible to accurately interpret the results and you won't be able to optimize the campaign at all. Keep your campaigns distinct between different products and for different purposes. The purpose of manual campaigns, then, is that you can be much more selective about what you're bidding on, and don't need to spend resources on keywords that don't serve you.

We recommend starting with an automatic campaign with a $2 bid level, then include the highest performing, or best converting keywords in a manual campaign with the following bid structure:

Broad match type: $2.2
Phrase match type: $2.4
Exact match type $2.6

Amazon will provide you with estimates for CPC bids, but we'd suggest you rely on your data more than you do on the estimates provided by Amazon.

***

How much to spend on Amazon PPC?

While most Amazon sellers need no extra convincing that PPC is a good idea, they do want to know how much they should be spending on ads. The truth is, you should be spending as much on ads as is profitable for you. If every dollar you spend on ads is producing $20 in sales, you probably want to push as many dollars through that pipeline as you possibly can.

Another factor is the competitiveness of your product category. In competitive categories like nutritional supplements, competitors are willing to place high bids on popular keywords, pushing the cost of advertising up as high as a few dollars per click. In other categories with less sophisticated competitors, the cost per click on some keywords can be just a few cents.

Still, it's helpful to have some guidelines in place around ad spend. Our PPC team spends every day setting up, analyzing, and optimizing Amazon PPC campaigns, and discovered a rule of thumb that helps sellers to estimate what their ad spend should be for Amazon Sponsored Products, which we call the 25/25 rule.

The 25/25 Rule of Amazon PPC Spend

Advertising Cost of Sales (ACoS) is the cost of your ad campaign relative to the sales that it generates. Let's say that you spend $250 on a PPC campaign in a week, which directly drove $1000 in product sales, your ACoS would be 25%. Ideally, your ACoS would always be in the 20 to 25% range. That's the comfort zone for an established, mature campaign in a category which is not overly competitive. Of course, if you can get it lower, that's great too.

Some accounts may have a lower overall ACoS if they are in less competitive categories, or if their competitors don't utilize PPC (or don't do it well). Conversely, brands in very competitive categories may struggle to get to a 25% average ACoS as some of the most lucrative and high-volume search terms are being aggressively bid against by other sellers.

Ideally, 25% of your sales would be sourced through PPC. This is the percentage of overall unit sales which are attributed to ad campaigns, as compared to organic sales in a given time period, such as a week or month. Anywhere from 15% to around 30-35% is the sweet spot.

Having less than 10% of your sales being attributed to PPC means you're running a very profitable campaign, but might be losing out on increased sales volume by bidding too conservatively and limiting your budget, or are using too small a set of keywords. Seeing a percentage of revenue from ads higher than 35% means you might be relying too heavily on paid advertising efforts to drive sales, and may want to examine increasing your rank organically for high-priority terms customers are using to find your product. The ideal scenario is to have your percent of sales from ads remain steady while watching your overall revenue grow month-to-month.

Ultimately, 25% of revenue attributed to advertising efforts is a happy medium between the two extremes — it's a good target to shoot for, and a sign of a healthy PPC account.

In terms of a hard dollar amount to spend each month on PPC, the minimum amount you can spend each day on Amazon Sponsored Product Ads is $5 (so you'll need to spend at least $150 a month on ads). From there, you can use the 25/25 heuristic to calculate an appropriate budget based on your target monthly revenue. If your target monthly revenue on Amazon is $20,000 per month, your projected spend using the 25/25 rule will be $1,250.

Total sales to be sourced from PPC: 25% of $20,000 = $5,000.
Target ACoS (25%) of $5,000 = $1,250

While wanting to know what you *should* spend is perfectly understandable, the question really should be *"what **can** I spend?"* It's not so much about the dollar amount you're putting in, as what you're getting back. Again, if you can put in a dollar into your advertising and get $10 or $20 back, you should put as many dollars in as you can, because it's going to pay off in droves.

Sales Attribution and Latency periods

Amazon's sales data changes over time – your ACoS for a given campaign may change from one day to the next. Due to the nature of how people shop on Amazon, the attribution is fairly fluid. Think about how people shop on Amazon. They might click through to a product and view it before adding it to their Wishlist. They may only add the product to their cart and check out several days later.

Troubleshooting your campaigns

With so many variables to take into consideration, plus extraneous effects like seasonality and what your competitors are up to (not to mention Amazon's constant system changes), it can be hard to know whether your campaigns are performing optimally. Here are some common mistakes that we see brands making with their PPC campaigns:

- Not using Auto campaigns, only using manual campaigns. This means missing good potential keywords that Amazon would have uncovered for you.
- Being impatient with campaigns. It takes time for campaigns to start producing results, and there's also a delay in reporting sales figures. Amazon recommends advertisers leave the campaigns running for 7 - 10 days before making any changes or pausing the campaigns. And at Bobsled, we operate on a 6-week campaign optimization cycle. Patience is key!
- Wasted spend: Spending too much and allowing bids to get too high.
- Running ads for interests rather than ASINs for Product Display Ads, leading to wasted spend.
- Eligibility. If a product is out of stock or you have lost the buy box to a competitor, Amazon will not run ads for that product.
- If you don't see clicks and impressions on a campaign, that is a red flag. This could mean errant negative keyword queries, Amazon has disallowed the ad campaign. The latter could be caused by Amazon disagreeing with the pricing of the product, as well as how relevant they see the ad being to your chosen search terms.
- Insufficient spend limits. Often brands will put daily or account-level spend limits in place in order to safeguard from over-spending. The issue arises when those limits are forgotten about or when the account grows beyond the spend limits.
- Your ads don't get any impressions. This either means that you're not bidding enough for that keyword or that it's an extremely niche product that Amazon is having trouble categorizing. The first problem is easily solved (you just bid more), but in the second case, you just have to keep an eye on it. It could take two or three weeks before the campaign actually displays any ads, so you have to be a patient and then optimize it as usual once it does start displaying.

The results from the campaigns depend on the campaign setup (optimizing bids, keywords and ads), and of course, the quality and desirability of the product. Keep in mind that sales data lags for up to 72 hours. This means that your campaigns may look fairly unsuccessful in their first days of running, don't get discouraged!

Display Advertising and AAP

Amazon Advertising Program (AAP) is built for larger brands who have dedicated brand marketing budgets, and are prepared to spend based on impressions rather than clicks (PPC).

Broadly speaking, AAP partially solves a problem that a lot of brands have with selling on Amazon: accessing and leveraging data to attract more shoppers.

Advertisers using the platform can access proprietary retail data at scale. Brands can see the full path to purchase from when a shopper first saw their ad online, to the next time, to when they eventually navigated to Amazon, and finally whether they purchased the brand's product or a competitor's.

There's also a lot more creative capability. Advertisers can use Amazon's own tested templates to drive traffic, or generate their own creative campaigns. AAP allows advertisers to place ads on the Amazon marketplace websites, their subsidiary sites (IMDB.com for example), as well as third party websites that are available on other third party exchanges, such as the Wall Street Journal.

Advanced audience targeting with AAP

AAP has advanced audience targeting capabilities that are lacking in the Amazon PPC offerings. Brands can remarket to customers who viewed a product but didn't buy, target by demographic, and even target customers who are viewing competitor products.

With their vast array of shopper purchase data, Amazon can identify 'In-Market Audiences' – shoppers who have signaled their intention to purchase a product in a certain category or sub-category through recent search, browse, or purchase behavior. There's also 'Lifestyle Segments' – users who regularly shop or view specific types of products.

Finally, there's the ability to positively or negatively target existing customers by adding a brand's customer list and adding a pixel to the brand's website. This way, a brand can either attract past customers to discover new products to purchase on Amazon, or conversely, ensure that customers buying on their ecommerce store are *never* targeted with Amazon ads.

Above: an AAP placement on Amazon.com

AAP requires a higher level of advertising spend than AMS or Sponsored Products, which can be as little as $5/day. If you're working with Amazon's managed service division, called Ecommerce Marketing, the initial spend commitment is in the ballpark of $35,000 over the first two months. Spend is allocated toward impressions (the number of users who viewed a given ad) and measured on a cost per thousand (CPM or cost per mil) basis. The CPM offered depends on a few factors including where the ads will display, for example on the Fire tablet, Amazon.com, or through a 3rd party ad exchange network. Amazon's internal team will handle all the setup, creative development, and reporting for you.

Since individual Sellers and Vendors cannot access AAP directly, the other option is to work with an advertising or media agency like Bobsled which is certified by AMG and has access to the platform.

Advertising Is Not A Set and Forget Strategy

Recently at Bobsled Marketing we performed an audit on the existing PPC campaigns of a new client, and found that instead of an ACoS of around 25%, their ACoS had blown up to over *1000%*. They were quite literally spending ten times as much as they were making per sale, because no one was watching their campaigns. Amazon is just one channel for this company, but this kind of uncontrolled spending would cripple a smaller business in a matter of weeks. At Bobsled Marketing we review every client's campaigns at least twice a week to be efficient and effective with ad spend. It's a very hands-on process to avoid this kind of blow-out. Of course, we fixed the ACoS for this new client immediately, so our partnership got off to a good start, but it's a good demonstration that you need to be diligent with monitoring advertising campaigns.

Just like any other marketing strategy, you have to approach advertising with patience and a willingness to experiment. Advertising is not a magic bullet that will instantly make you money — you have to take the time to find out what works, track all your campaigns diligently, analyse the data and constantly make small iterations to optimize your campaigns.

Chapter Eight: Best Practices and General Know-How

While the market potential for Amazon sellers is obviously very high, there are also multiple opportunities for you to capitalize on within Amazon's ecosystem. Foremost among these are optimizing your account so that you can win the Buy Box more frequently compared to other sellers listing your products, getting involved in Lightning Deals, and taking a strategic approach to seasonal sales events.

Winning the Buy Box

"Winning the Buy Box" is the process by which your offer is assessed by Amazon's algorithm as the best option for the customer when multiple sellers are listing the same item. Winning the Buy Box is just Amazon's way of saying that you win the purchasing click from the customer.

So, no matter how many sellers are offering the same item, there will only be one listing for it on the Amazon marketplace. The seller who is currently winning the Buy Box, then, has *their* price displayed on the listing, so when a customer clicks 'Add to Cart', they get that particular price. Now, they *could* buy from a different seller if they decided to — all the other sellers (who are not currently winning the Buy Box) will be listed in a sidebar on the right-hand side of the product page, along with their prices and ratings (as you saw in the image in Chapter Three).

When there are multiple sellers of the same product, Amazon has to have a way to figure out who should get the sale. For example, if there are 10 sellers of a product, and they all have different offers (such as different prices or fulfillment terms), who should win the sale? To solve this, Amazon uses their search algorithm to prioritize relevance, sales velocity and conversion metrics, as well as to compare whether an offer is eligible for Prime (i.e. an FBA seller fulfilling through the Prime program, or Amazon themselves fulfilling through the Vendor program). Amazon will often win the sale if they have an offer on the product.

Another factor is price: the lowest priced offer will often win the sale, though not always. The other element that contributes to the algorithm is seller reputation — the length of time that seller has been active on Amazon, relative to competing sellers, and their overall feedback scores and success rates. These are each of the factors that we currently understand as contributing to who wins the Buy Box. If other Sellers are selling your product, it's important that you give yourself the best chance of winning every sale. You can do this by adjusting your prices, soliciting more positive seller feedback and customer reviews, and optimizing your fulfillment processes.

Now, while price is not the only factor, it *is* an important one. Seller tenure and reputation maintain an important role in the algorithm. If Seller A has only been on Amazon for a few weeks, has a handful of reviews and is offering a product at $30 (when Sellers B through F are selling it at $35), Seller A would probably still not win the Buy Box. If Seller A had been on Amazon for a few years, though, and has plenty of reviews, they most probably *would* win it.

Sellers with large product catalogs do not want to be sitting on Amazon, adjusting their prices all day to increase their chances of winning the Buy Box. Fortunately, there is repricing software available that will automatically adjust the prices of your products for you, based on rules that you determine. For example, you could set the price to always stay above a particular dollar amount, and that you don't want repricing to happen more often than five times a day. This would ensure that your pricing is optimized for competitiveness, without ending up in a 'race to the bottom'.

Amazon has also recently released their own repricing tool within Seller Central. From what we've seen up to the time of writing, this is not as robust an option as the third-party tools. You can't set the parameters as extensively as with other tools, so it can lead to uncompetitive, unprofitable pricing on your catalog.

How to Improve Your Seller Rating To Increase Your Buy Box Frequency

We've already talked about how critical positive reviews are to increasing your sales on Amazon, but seller feedback is also a powerful contributor. This is meant to be customers giving feedback on their direct experience with the seller. Now, the reality is that if you're using FBA, you won't have much interaction with your customers from a order fulfillment standpoint. You don't have tracking numbers, don't have control of the delivery timeframe, and there's not much you can do to impact the customer's experience, but there is still this customer feedback metric to measure up to. Customers can write reviews and rate sellers after the sale, just like they can with product reviews. The difference is that the seller feedback only displays when the customer clicks through to your seller profile, so you do have to create a balancing act between obtaining product reviews (which help with product conversions) and seller feedback (which helps with winning the Buy Box). We recommend following up with a certain percentage of customers to ask them to leave a Seller Review, so as to round out your metrics.

Seasonal Sales Events and Holidays

The fourth quarter of the year is, of course, the biggest time of the year for anyone in retail. In 2017, Amazon saw incredible growth in Q4. Record number of units shipped worldwide with Amazon Prime, more than four million customers joined Prime (either through free trails or paid memberships) in one week alone and Prime members shopped more than 100,000 Lightning Deals on Amazon.com with Prime Early Access. Items shipped for free more than doubled during the 2017 holiday season and the last Prime Now order was delivered in time for Christmas in 58 minutes at 11:58 p.m. on Christmas Eve in Baltimore, MD.

Needless to say, they expect the same thing to happen in the holiday seasons of 2018 and beyond, so here at Bobsled we've put together an extensive strategy to help our clients make the most of this important time of year. We really recommend that you spend all of Q3 prepping for Q4, because the further in advance you are prepared, the more capable you will be of capitalizing on opportunities as they arise.

Get Ready Early

The data clearly shows that customers want Prime during the holiday season, so keeping consistent, healthy FBA inventory is critical for making your own Q4 one for the record books.

We've covered the importance of knowing your inventory timelines in earlier chapters, but this becomes even more important during the holidays. Amazon is receiving *millions* of units of inventory during this time, so by preparing your inventory and beginning the shipping process in September, you won't get caught up in the glut of sellers frantically scrambling to get their inventory into fulfillment centers in November and December. If you're using FBA, apply for increased inventory limits to make space for additional units if necessary. This can take anywhere from a few seconds to a couple of days to be approved, depending on your seller history.

Have your FBA shipping plans set up and ready to go before the end of Q3, and when possible, sticker your inventory with your FNSKUs (Amazon's internal barcode labelling system). This will save you some money as Amazon charges $0.20 per unit stickered, your shipment will be processed through Receiving at Fulfillment Centers much faster, making your products ready for purchase sooner. And, you avoid having Amazon incorrectly sticker your products, which can otherwise cause increased delays, returns and stress at a time of year when no one needs any more of that!

Run Promotions

This is the ideal time of year to run promotions. You can increase traffic to your product pages significantly by developing product promotion plans. Consider quantity discounts or cross-selling discounts with other items in your Amazon catalog.

Coupons

Some brands include inserts in their product packaging to encourage repeat purchasing. Again, you want to play by the rules, and avoid encouraging people to go straight to your site. You might invite them to follow you on social media or to take an action that's not specifically directing them to make their next purchase off Amazon. Alternately, you could include a 'next purchase' coupon or incentive on your inserts for a period of time to encourage repeat purchasing. This would work particularly well leading up to holiday seasons — for example, offering coupon codes on your packaging insert collateral for all of Q3 for customers to use the coupon in Q4 when they are buying holiday gifts or end-of-year stockpiling.

Lightning Deals

Lightning Deals can be a great way to bring visibility to your products and boost your overall performance over the holidays. If you're eligible for Lightning Deals, make sure you take advantage of them and offer as many of your products as you can, and making it appealing for customers who arrive after the deal to buy as much as possible.

Lightning Deals are promotions that Amazon offers sellers who have been on the platform for a while (they don't say how long you have to be selling for, but internally at Bobsled we think it's probably a couple of months at a minimum). You submit a deal, offering a discount on a particular item or collection, which Amazon promotes extensively for four to twelve hours across the platform. These deals can bring you a ton of traffic and sales — we've had clients see sales increases of up to 30 times their usual amount. This really helps with your Best Seller Rank (your organic sales rank among products in your category). For a period of time, your sales rank will be better, and so you'll get more full-priced sales after the Lightning Deal ends. It's an excellent way to liquidate inventory, and to get attention for your products. Since so many people are buying your products, you could also expect a small percentage of them to write reviews.

In order for you to run a Lightning Deal, Amazon will recommend products for you to submit. It could be multiple products from your catalog, and you can confirm which of those selected SKUs you want to offer a deal for. We've found that the more products you select, the more likely Amazon is to accept the deal — they're less likely to invest as many resources if you're only offering one product, so try to accept as many of the recommended offers Amazon gives you, in order to give yourself the best shot of having your Lightning Deal approved.

After selecting which products to include in Lightning Deals, you choose the week that you want the Lightning Deal to run. For example, you might select to run the deal four weeks from now, because you know that your inventory will be ready by then. So you choose the week, but Amazon will choose the day and time. They will notify you of the specific date and time 2 weeks before your scheduled deal week.

If you do a Lightning Deal, make sure you have lots of inventory. This means you can get the most out of the promotion, and get the most out of the halo period after the promotion, where people are buying your products at full price. You want to send in at least 5 times the amount of inventory you would normally expect to go through in a week, and to give yourself enough time with your normal delivery schedules to get all the inventory delivered and processed at Amazon's fulfillment centers.

If Amazon runs your deal at a low-traffic time (e.g. 2AM on a weekday), you may not experience as much of a lift as you would if they ran the deal at 2PM on a Saturday, for example. Customers also favor steep discounts where they feel that they're getting a good deal, so the bigger the discount, the better your Lightning Deal will generally perform.

There are two ways to create and submit a Lightning Deal, you can either 1) Go to the Lightning Deals Dashboard to create and submit a deal, allowing you to select a product and set the price, quantity, schedule, and any product variations or 2) See all eligible products in the Lightning Deals Dashboard. Eligible products are automatically displayed when they meet certain criteria such as quality (products must have a sales history on Amazon and at least a 3 star rating, this can change by marketplace and the time of year), product variation (deals should include as many product variations as possible), category (products such as alcohol, e-cigarettes, medical devices are not eligible), fulfillment method (must be Prime eligible in all states), condition (only new condition products) and seller feedback rating (must receive a minimum of 5 ratings per month and have at least an overall 3.5-star rating, this can change by marketplace and the time of year). If any more criteria becomes apparent, we'll add it to the Resources Page (http://www.bobsledmarketing.com/amazon-expansion-plan-resources) for this book.

Bundles

Creating bundles and multi-packs are another great option at this time of year. Bundles are packs of products that are used together or are highly complementary.

For example, a Bobsled client sells spice mixes on Amazon, and so they might offer a bundle of different kinds of steak spices, or a bundle of Thanksgiving-specific spices. Those options could be bundled with a spice rack or a spice grinder, to be given as a gift or as a convenient way to prepare your family's holiday meals. Not only is it a great offer for the customer, but it's an easy way to increase your average order value, particularly if you are selling lower-priced items. You can bundle as many items together as you want, as long as they're complimentary.

You can also offer multi-packs, which often perform really well. It might be a 2-pack or a 20-pack — you can sell it at a higher price point while providing a good value to the customer. Multi-packs tend to perform best when listed as a variation on the product page. For example, if you look at the product page for a particular label-maker, you'll see that you can buy a single unit, or you can buy two, or three (and if you have a warehouse where you'll be doing a lot of labelling, then you're going to buy the multi-pack).

(You should note that bundles and multi-packs need to be packaged together before they are sent to Amazon. Amazon will not put these together for you in their warehouses, so again, if you plan to use this strategy for the Q4 rush, make sure you've planned it early enough to make all the necessary adjustments in your own production and packaging timelines. You will also need to have a separate UPC code and SKU for each of the bundles and multi-packs.)

PPC Ads and Page Optimization

You should also run PPC ads, since an efficient, targeted ad campaign is a strategic way to direct customer attention to your products and can help increase traffic and conversions. Ideally, you would get campaigns up and running two to three weeks before an event or holiday (e.g. Thanksgiving, Black Friday, Jewish Holidays, Christmas, New Year as relevant), and revisit your back-end keywords to ensure the highest volume search terms are included in your listings. Evaluate your product titles to ensure they are keyword-rich and highlight your products as a great holiday gift. You might even consider increasing your daily spend for specific campaigns if your analytics indicate that those campaigns are likely to attribute to your growth over the holiday season.

You can also make holiday-specific updates to product pages. When customers land on your product pages, you want to ensure that the bullet points, description, and images inspire them to click 'Add to Cart'. Audit your product pages, so that they are in tip-top form for the season ahead, as well as including holiday-specific images of your products. If you have attractive gift boxes that your products come in, or appealing arrangements for bundled products, make sure those are on display so that they are eye-catching and will help convert browsers into buyers.

Seasonal Pricing

Rounding out the list of 'must-dos' is assessing the competitor landscape to see where your prices fall in relation to similar products. This is the final, essential piece of the puzzle and will give you the greatest insight about the quarter to come. By benchmarking your prices with your closest competitors — particularly during the holiday season — you keep a tight grip on your particular market and a stronger sense of how you can get a competitive edge.

The year-end holidays are definitely the main event when it comes to selling online, but there are seasonal sales events that happen all throughout the year:

- Valentine's Day
- Mother's Day
- July 4th
- Father's Day
- Back to School
- Prime Day
- Thanksgiving
- Black Friday

- Cyber Monday

Prime Day, Black Friday and Cyber Monday are other major sales events that you need to be prepared for, and I would recommend taking a similar approach to these events as outlined above for the year-end holidays. The other events are much more influenced by category, so it's up to you to identify which holidays or large events are likely to create a surge in sales and to prepare accordingly. For example, if you sell jewellery, then Valentine's Day will present a big opportunity for you, but if you sell office supplies, it probably won't.

Regardless of your category, the biggest mistake you can make at this time is not having enough inventory available. If you run out of a popular item a few weeks before Christmas, it's extremely unlikely that it will be received, processed and made available for sale again during the buying rush. It's better to send more inventory than you think you will need and then deal with any surplus afterwards (and you may be pleasantly surprised to find that you don't end up with any surplus).

Key Dates

Towards the end of the year, there's a spate of buying events that you need to be prepared for, each of which show substantial Year On Year (YOY) growth in the ecommerce space.

- Thanksgiving Day; 24% YOY increase in 2017. Thanksgiving Day saw the highest YOY increase in overall gross merchandise volume (sale price charged to the customer multiplied by the number of items sold)

- Black Friday; 22% YOY growth

- Cyber Sunday; 22% YOY growth

- Cyber Monday; 18% YOY growth

- Boxing Day: traditional shopping holiday for UK and Canadian markets

To-Do: September Checklist

September is when a lot of the 'heavy lifting' needs to happen in order for your business to be ready for the holiday season.

- Start planning:
    - Take time to analyze your Q4 performance from last year. What went right and wrong last year? Start a plan to maximize festive success this year.

- Consider a hybrid model:
    - If you sell on the Vendor Central or Vendor Express platforms, consider adopting a hybrid approach by opening a Seller Central account and leveraging the FBA program in addition to filling Vendor POs. This can ensure that there is enough available inventory over the holidays, and that all of the product variations in your assortment are represented, not just the ones that Amazon sees as being high-potential.

- Ship inventory:
    - This is the final month before the official start of the Fourth Quarter. Ship your inventory in September so your inventory doesn't get caught in the traffic jam of inbound shipments to Amazon Fulfillment Centers.

- Keyword research:
    - Spend some time researching your potential Amazon search terms, finding the most relevant words for each product listing to enhance your product's visibility. Use this research to update back-end keyword metadata and experiment with updated product titles.

To-Do: October Checklist

October is the time to consolidate your service model, and make final tweaks to product listings to maximize conversions.

- Product and ad display audit:
  - Check to see how your Sponsored Product ads & product listings display in mobile search results.

- Update product titles:
  - Leverage keyword research and also use the brand terms and other words people are searching with. Be sure to put the most important information in the first 25 characters of your titles.

- Update product images:
  - Are your product images good quality? Conduct an audit to make sure all images are high resolution and optimized for each channel, consider experimenting with dynamic or alternative angles to stand out from competitors.

- Beef up customer service capabilities:
  - Are you responding to customers on weekends? If not, you could be hurting your metrics. Around this time, Amazon also asks merchants to respond to customers within 12 hours (instead of the usual 24 hours) in order to create the best customer experience. At busy times, don't forget to monitor all of your feedback metrics and deal with customer queries and complaints quickly.

To-Do: November Checklist

It's all about PPC ("Pay Per Click" advertising) this month. This is how you start driving high volumes of eager-to-buy traffic to your store.

PPC Checklist:

- PPC campaigns need to be running for two to three weeks before an event or holiday.
    - For example, Black Friday PPC campaigns should be set up in early November. Use negative keywords. Save money and boost performance by eliminating keywords you don't want to target.

- Start increasing bids for holiday keywords slowly and track progress.

- Two weeks before Black Friday: Upload Black Friday PPC ads in "paused" status.

- Even if you're using automatic bidding, make sure you check in on the peak days to make sure your bids are working as they should. If they're not, reevaluate them while in progress.

- If selling in Canada, the UK or other international territories, start ramping up PPC in those marketplaces in mid-November as well, to prepare for the peak December shopping period.

To-Do: December and January Checklist

There's actually less to do *during* the holiday period, except to handle customer support.

December:

- Prepare for Boxing Day if you sell in the UK or Canada. Prepare keyword-specific campaigns for this holiday and social campaigns for Boxing Day, keep them paused until Christmas.

- Prepare for a Post-Christmas inventory clean-up.

- Launch any post-holiday sales to take advantage of consumer looking for deals or returning gifts. This activity extends right into January.

January

- Be aggressive with Lightning Deals and other promotions to help clear excess inventory left over from the holidays to save on inventory storage fees in the coming months.

- Deals and promotions can also help attract the millions of consumers who will want to be spending the gift cards that they received for Christmas.

International Trends To Be Aware Of

United Kingdom:

Boxing Day (December 26th) is a national holiday and the traditional bargain-hunting day for Britons. Since better sales are expected *after* Christmas rather than before, the bulk of holiday shopping spend happens in December for Brits, rather than throughout November and December in the US. Still, Black Friday is emerging as a major shopping event, though this is not a public holiday as it is in the US.

Canada:

Black Friday and Cyber Monday aren't as big a deal in Canada as they are in the US, and most shopping actually happens in the month of December. Like in the UK, Boxing Day (December 26th) is a national holiday and the traditional bargain-hunting day for Canadians. Since better sales are expected *after* Christmas rather than before, the bulk of holiday shopping spend for Canadians happens in December, rather than throughout November and December as in the US.

Chapter Nine: International Expansion

The US is, at this time, the biggest consumer market in the Western world. Sales outside of North America represented around 30-35% of Amazon's total worldwide sales. Amazon's American marketplace, then, is the best place for retail brands to be in order to get the most 'bang for their buck' when they're developing their online sales presence. If you are a US-based brand, there is only one reason that you would expand into Amazon's international marketplaces before you had capped out your American potential, and that's if you're in a highly competitive category that is less crowded in other territories. Besides that exception, I strongly recommend maximizing your US seller account before expanding.

(If your company is an international retail brand from Europe, Asia, or Australia, and you're looking to grow quickly, it's my recommendation that the US is the first market you launch in. This is simply due to the size and established infrastructure in the US — with a population of over 318 million people, no other retail market can provide the same level of opportunity.)

It's important to understand that most of the other territories Amazon is operating in have much smaller populations than the US. If you're looking at Canada, for example, they have 10% of the population of the US, so the most you're going to get is a 5-10% lift from going into that market, even though it's a relatively easy logistical exercise.

Active Amazon Sellers (those with at least one Seller Feedback review in the past month)

Market	Active Amazon Sellers
United States	208,577
United Kingdom	66,175
Germany	62,816

Japan	51,853
France	38,644
Italy	37,319
Spain	29,292
Canada	28,842
India	22,175
Australia	1,519
Mexico	1,291
China	1,025
Brazil (Books & Electronics only, as of March 2018)	443

Source: Marketplace Pulse, February 2018

That said, with high competition products, the barriers to entry are a little bit higher in international markets, which means that your competitors may be delaying their own expansion into fresh territories. If you can get an edge by being one of the first brands in your category to have an international Amazon strategy, you will be building something defensible down the line. European markets are particularly attractive, thanks to the strong economic performance of the region, and Asian markets are seeing remarkable growth as the economies gain momentum and individual disposable incomes increase.

In this section, we're going to take a high-level view of the opportunity and logistics of expanding into each new territory. Note that we get deep into the details of everything happening in these international marketplaces on the Resources Page (http://www.bobsledmarketing.com/amazon-expansion-plan-resources) on our website, so check back periodically to keep up to date with what's happening in your target territories.

European Markets

Once you've maximized your presence in the US market, the two most attractive markets to expand to are the UK and Germany, followed by France, Italy and Spain. These countries are close enough to be treated by Amazon as a single marketplace, both in terms of offering a single Seller or Vendor account for all markets, and in offering consolidated fulfillment options. As a result, Marketplace Pulse reports that over half of European sellers have products listed on more than one EU marketplace.

There is quite a lot of overlap in the process for getting set up in the UK and Germany, so if your logistics can handle the increase in demand, it's a faster way to expand.

United Kingdom

- The UK, obviously, is appealing because all the language requirements are in English, so you already have all your product copy, keywords, your emails, and product packaging. Shoppers in the UK have adapted to ecommerce and we see continued growth projections for ecommerce markets within the UK.

- There is consistent, significant growth seen on Amazon in the UK. While Amazon does not release information about the number of shoppers or Prime members in each country marketplace, we do know that there are around 60,000 active sellers on Amazon.co.uk today, compared with 49,000 in 2016.

- The process and requirements for exporting to the UK are intermediate. Sellers need to apply for VAT (Value Added Tax) and EORI numbers and the application processes can take around five weeks.

- Import fees, duties and taxes, as well as consumption taxes, are also intermediate when compared with the other markets.

- Amazon's weight handling fees in the UK market are higher than in the US, due to higher overall costs of logistics in the country. (This is true for pretty much every market outside the US — we are spoiled here with very low shipping and labor costs compared with most developed countries.)

Germany

- With a population of 82.7 million compared with the US' 325.7 million, total ecommerce sales in Germany are 15% of what it is in the US ($68 billion versus $453 billion in the US).

- There is consistent, significant growth seen on Amazon in Germany. While Amazon does not release information about the number of shoppers or Prime members in each country marketplace, we do know that there are around 50,000 active sellers on Amazon.co.de today, compared with 40,000 in 2016.

- The process and requirements for exporting to Germany are intermediate and are quite similar to those of the UK.

- Import fees, duties and taxes, as well as consumption taxes, are on the medium side when compared with the other markets; they are slightly higher than those of the UK.

- Amazon's weight handling and inventory storage fees in the German market are also higher than in the US, due to higher overall costs of logistics in the country.

Germany actually has the second biggest Amazon marketplace after the US. There's a little more complexity to establishing your brand there, because you have to have your product listings translated into German, do keyword research and PPC campaigns in German, you need to provide customer service and VAT invoices in German, and ideally you would have product packaging in German too. The packaging is not strictly required, but it will create a much better customer experience, which leads to better repurchase rates and reviews — we recommend professional translations right from the beginning so that you have as much of an advantage coming into the market as possible.

Other European Markets

The European Fulfilment Network and Pan-European Inventory programs (these fulfillment options are discussed in more detail below) mean that you can establish a presence in all those countries fairly easily, without having to keep your inventory in each country. If you're going to be looking at European countries outside of Germany and the UK, it's worth looking at all of them — it's most interesting in aggregate, since the markets are small relative to the US.

Distributing Your Products Throughout Europe

European Seller Account

This account allows you to have all your European marketplace listings available in one dashboard: you don't have to create separate accounts for Amazon France, Amazon Spain, Amazon Germany and so on. It's all available on the same interface, and all the sales from all territories are tracked in the same place. You still need to manually create listings and offers in each country — you don't just set up Product A and have it automatically show up in all the marketplaces you want to sell it in. But once you've obtained your VAT number and have been approved to open an account for Europe and the UK, you can manage all your listings for all those territories in one place.

EFN, Pan-European and Multi-Country Fulfillment

The difference between the three options is how and where your inventory is stored.

The Multi-Country option is where you decide how much inventory is going to be held in each country and you are responsible for exporting it there. If you want to have 25% of your inventory for a particular SKU in France, 25% in Spain, and 50% in Germany, you're responsible for moving that inventory around between those territories and maintaining your inventory levels. The key benefits of this option are:

a) The products are Prime-eligible. Since the inventory is available in the customer's home country, they get it within two days and don't pay any extra shipping fees. As we know, Prime eligibility can help increase product sales quite dramatically.
b) Control over inventory levels in each country. You can ensure that there is adequate stock available in the countries which you sell in, and only sell in the countries which are strategically important to you.

The downside to this option is higher costs associated with importing and transporting inventory to each country that you wish to sell in. This option is better suited for retailers with large amounts of inventory and that have an expertise in forecasting sales across Europe.

The European Fulfilment Network is where you have all of your inventory stored in the UK but that product is also available to purchase in other markets. The benefit of this option is that you don't have to handle the logistics of moving inventory all over Europe all the time — Amazon does it for you. The downside to this option is that your products won't be Prime-eligible outside of the UK. This means that the customer has to wait a bit longer to receive the product and may have to pay additional shipping fees — factors which will likely dampen your sales in those markets. This option is better suited for smaller sellers with lower levels of inventory.

The Pan-European program is a new addition to the mix. Amazon moves your inventory around the different markets for free, so you don't have to pay to export or ship your products around, but you also don't get to choose how much inventory is moved into each market. This is determined by Amazon's demand algorithms — they will predict how much product will sell in a particular territory in a particular amount of time, and will shift your inventory around accordingly. The benefit to this program is obviously that Amazon covers the cost of moving inventory around, and also that your products would be Prime-eligible in each market where inventory is held. The downside to this option is that you don't get to choose where your inventory is relocated to, and in what quantity. If Amazon anticipates low demand for some products, they may not relocate any inventory at all. This option is better suited for sellers with larger amounts of inventory and an interest in targeting Europe without the expertise or resources to forecast inventory in each country.

North American Markets

Canada

- There is fast growth being seen on Amazon in Canada. While Amazon does not release information about the number of shoppers or Prime members in each country marketplace, we do know that 25,100 sellers joined the Amazon.ca marketplace this year. This equals 174 new sellers every day.

- The process and requirements for exporting to Canada are intermediate. Sellers would organize as a NRI (non-resident importer) which has no local incorporation requirement, but the various registration numbers will involve an application process of six weeks or more.

- Import fees, duties and taxes, as well as consumption taxes, are slightly lower than the other markets.

- Amazon's FBA fulfillment fees in the Canadian market are also higher than in the US, due to higher overall costs of logistics in the country.

Mexico

In 2015, Amazon made its first considerable attempt to break into Mexico, as it launched a Spanish website and established a fulfillment center outside of Mexico City. Amazon has been selling its Kindle e-books in Mexico since 2013, but it has built only one fulfillment center.

The process and requirements for exporting to Mexico are onerous compared with the markets like Canada, the UK, or those within the EU. This is a territory that has some export challenges, and you will really need to work with an agent there. It's recommended that Mexico is explored as a growth market only after other markets have been scaled up.

North America Unified Account

This is the same concept as the European Seller Account: it keeps your American, Canadian and Mexican accounts in the same dashboard for easy management. If you want to have product listings in each of those markets, again, you need to create them all manually.

Asia Pacific Markets

Many markets in Asia are growing rapidly, and creating plenty of opportunity as they do. We frequently get questions about Australia, Japan, China, India and South-East Asian countries, and each of them is worth delving into here.

Australia

As an Australian native myself, I was very excited with Amazon announced its plans to launch down under. Australians are digitally savvy online shoppers already, but there is not the same abundance of selection locally. So many consumers end up buying products from overseas even with exorbitant shipping fees to get an item from one side of the world to another.

Unfortunately Amazon seemed to rush its launch in Australia, offering a limited selection and no Prime shipping program. As of the time of writing, there is still no FBA option for sellers and no Prime delivery option for shoppers.

I do believe that Australia will become a significant market for Amazon and for brands who sell there. Although it is a relatively small population, about 40% smaller than Canada, residents have high average disposable incomes and are avid followers of international trends. My agency, Bobsled Marketing, will be actively supporting brands who want to launch in Australia.

Japan

Japan is the Asian territory we get the most interest in, but it's also one of the most difficult territories to get clear data on. Unless you have an entity and an agent in Japan, it has historically been very difficult for companies to export products there. You need to have an agent (who must be a Japanese resident) to clear your products through customs. The process is much more onerous than it is in other territories, because the entity that is importing the goods holds all the product liability. So for example, if your product is a kitchen appliance that has a faulty element and ends up injuring people, the importer is responsible for any claims, rather than the manufacturer or the retailer that purchased the goods to sell.

There are also the usual logistical challenges. While Amazon has made this aspect much easier, it remains to be seen how it's going to work over the next few years, without requiring brands to set up an entirely new legal entity in Japan solely for the purposes of testing out the marketing.

China

Amazon has struggled to gain a footing in China. They have a very small percentage of the market share. China is an attractive market for a lot of US brands — especially skincare and baby products — high-income Chinese consumers often don't trust products manufactured domestically. Anything related to baby care, natural or organic skincare or luxury items are much more prized when purchased from verified US brands. It does remain to be seen, though, whether Amazon is the best marketplace for this. At this point in time, if you are determined to expand into China, you may be better served choosing a different platform to start out with. TaoBao, JD.com, and AliBaba have much more significant market penetration than Amazon in China.

India

Based on pure size, India is Amazon's biggest emerging opportunity. But India has complex regulatory requirements that make it difficult to replicate the exact same distribution playbook as in established markets. Government regulations mean that there's no Vendor Program there — it's all third-party merchants, because marketplace sellers are required be completely independent of the marketplace owner.

This is a market that historically has been a difficult territory for ecommerce because of the urban planning, but it's emerging as a high-opportunity (if high-complexity) market. This means that Amazon has to come up with a localized strategy that makes it easy for new sellers to get the benefits of its platform without worrying about the regulatory hurdles. Amazon made a $2 billion in investment in the country to launch there, and analysts who follow the retailer believe they will keep investing in the marketplace to edge out other competitors such as Flipkart.

Logistical Considerations for All New Territories

If your products require usage instructions, you can update your current branding materials to include instructions in multiple languages, so that it's ready to use in any territory you expand to. As you're getting set up, it's worth thinking long-term — maybe your external packaging is in English, but you can have inserts and instructions in the local language or multiple languages to ensure that it's easy for customers everywhere to use the product immediately.

This approach also keeps your logistical complexity to a minimum. Not only is it costly to print and package multiple variations of all your products, it requires a lot more time and attention at the fulfillment level. You don't want to run into inventory issues because your fulfillment team can't find the Spanish inventory, or mistakenly send German inventory to Portugal.

It does depend on the product: for example, a skincare cream might have the insert in the local language, but the customer is unlikely to hold onto that. The customer experience, then, is potentially impacted by not having the label with instructions in their local language. Compared to a piece of furniture, which you only assemble once and then never need the instructions for again, it can be a very different outcome and experience for the customer.

Another best practice is to consider setting up unique SKU IDs for each marketplace (as the variant structure is different in each territory). So red-XL-tshirt might become red-XL-tshirt-UK. This is so that Amazon recognizes your international listings as separate to the US listings and can prevent some issues with product listing information being merged. The UPC / EAN (barcodes) can remain the same in each marketplace, though.

You need to have someone online (either a contractor or employee) who can provide multilingual customer support. There also are pretty good online translation services available now. Most have an automated aspect, but some also allow a final review by local native speakers. Leveraging hybrid translation services like these allow you to have an English-speaking customer service rep handling all the incoming and outgoing inquiries, keeping the timeline to just a couple of hours, with the messages reviewed by a native speaker in the meantime. This means that you don't necessarily have to have someone on your team that speaks the language of the territories you are expanding into.

You can also hire an agency that will handle the launch and strategic aspects of international marketplace expansions, as well as the administrative and operational aspects of the day to day processes managing multiple marketplaces. This is part of our process at Bobsled Marketing — at the same time that we're launching your store into new territories, we also run the systems that ensure everything operates smoothly and without disruption. It's a done for you service: a complete product launch and channel management service. If you're in Spain, France, Germany, UK — we'll provide customer support for all those accounts. We have a team of people who can help you handle all your marketing and customer support needs in multiple territories.

Chapter Ten: VAT for European Territories and GST in Canada

VAT — the Value Added Tax — is similar in concept to the American state sales tax. It's applicable throughout the UK and Europe, and functions as a consumption tax that companies collect from customers at the point of sale, on behalf of the government, and remit to the government quarterly. When sending the invoice or receipt to customers, VAT should always be listed as a separate line item to the sale price. The amount that VAT is charged at varies between territories — it's a flat 20% in the UK, and is between 17-27% between the various European states.

When you begin the process of expanding into European markets, one of the first things you need to do is get a VAT number assigned to your business for each country. In order to apply for a European Amazon account, you need to already have a VAT number, and Amazon will take a few days to verify that your VAT number is valid (you can't just enter a string of numbers and hope they won't check it!).

VAT is calculated on the value of the item, any international shipping costs, the value of any import duties, and the value of any insurance that you put on the item. VAT is a comprehensive tax in that sense — everything that you need to remit to the government of that territory is processed through the VAT.

Because you need a different VAT number for each territory throughout the UK and Europe, you need to apply at the relevant governing office in each country. At the time of writing, the processing time to get your VAT in each territory is between five and six weeks. If you plan to expand into multiple territories at once, then, you should apply for all your VAT numbers around the same time, so that your stores can all launch concurrently. If you're taking your expansion a little slower, then you can simply apply for one territory at a time and factor the processing time into any future decisions.

Regardless of how quickly you plan to expand, we recommend dealing with a local tax accountant in each territory, because you need to have a locally registered agent who can file your quarterly taxes for you. You have to physically file each quarter, *and* the tax body of the territory might pay a visit to the location listed in your VAT application. Having an accountant with a physical location in the country, who handles all of this for you, will ensure that any audits or visits go smoothly and that any misunderstandings or problems are avoided. It might cost a few hundred dollars to engage the accountant to set up the VAT, and a couple hundred more per quarter to have them file all the taxes for you, but it's a very affordable insurance policy to ensure you're compliant with the tax requirements of that country.

In order to be approved for a VAT number, you will need to provide a few pieces of information. You'll be asked for some banking information, details about the nature of your business, as well as providing proof of personal identity of the president of the company or equivalent, and proof of your business address.

Once you receive your VAT number, you can set up your Amazon account for that territory. When you open the account, you'll be asked to list your VAT number, and this will automatically add the VAT amount to each purchase made through your store. You don't have to go through any additional steps to make sure that it's collected correctly. That part of the process is simple, but actually remitting the VAT amount is not so straightforward, and this is where having a local accountant really pays off.

They will go through all of your records each quarter, calculate the amount you owe, and submit all the necessary paperwork and payments to the tax office. They will understand the international regulations and they'll make sure that your remittances are done correctly. It's really not worth trying to 'wing it' when dealing with international taxation processes — it's too complex and comes with too much risk. It's critical to partner with someone who can handle all this smoothly for you.

Canada's consumption tax — GST, or Goods and Services Tax — functions in much the same way. You apply for the number through the Canadian tax office, and it currently takes about six to eight weeks to get approved and get your GST number. While the general GST rate is fixed at 5%, there are variations in taxation rates between the provinces, which you can find in the Canada section of our Resources Page (http://www.bobsledmarketing.com/amazon-expansion-plan-resources).

Here's a rough timeline you can refer to when preparing to apply for your VAT, Business Registration Number and Brand Registry:

Set up VAT Number (UK & Europe), Business Registration Number (Canada)

- VAT: Five to six weeks
- BRN: Six to eight weeks

Set up Amazon account in local marketplace

- UK / Europe: One day
- Canada: One day

Apply for Brand Registry

- Should happen as soon as you have your BRN
- Takes anywhere from several days to several weeks depending on the product category and what records Amazon asks for

Mechanisms For Getting Paid

Amazon has its own native currency conversion program (creatively named Amazon Conversion Services) to handle cross-currency transactions. For example, if your customers are buying your products in pounds, but if you have an American bank account listed for your European stores, Amazon will convert that payment back into US dollars and deposit it into that account. That certainly makes getting paid very easy, but they don't have the best exchange rate.

If you're doing a lot of volume off-shore, even one or two percentage points on the conversion rate can add up to a large amount of revenue over time, so you may want to consider third-party currency services. A good example is Payoneer, which has more competitive rates than the native Amazon Currency Conversion service. There is an extra step involved in opening your account with them and having it integrated into your Amazon account, but once you're set up it can save you a lot of additional money. They function as a financial interface between you and Amazon, setting up a local bank account for you in the territory you're selling in where all payments from that territory will be deposited in the local currency. Then they do their own currency conversion at the more competitive rate and transfer the converted US dollars (or whatever your home currency is) into your original bank account.

You can set up an Amazon account that is linked to a local account in almost every country — they support almost all currencies, so you should be fine regardless of where you're getting set up.

Offshore Entities

This is a question that comes up frequently when people are looking to expand from the US into other countries, or from other countries into the US.

To sell in the US, you don't need an American business entity. You can function as an individual, a corporation, or any kind of legal entity outside of the US. When you set up your Amazon account, you go through a tax questionnaire which determines where you are located and drives you to fill out an IRS form that certifies that you are a non-US entity.

It's the same thing in Europe and the UK — you don't need to set up a local entity, all you need to do is set up your VAT number to comply with the consumption tax requirement. The only country where you do need to have a local entity, unless you have a robust agreement with a local agent, is Japan.

One caveat when talking about international trade is that each company's situation is different. International trade and taxation are highly complex areas, and for some businesses, there may be advantages to having offshore entities to manage the international aspects of the business. We are not tax experts, though, and you should discuss this area in detail with your tax accountant to find out what the best course of action is for you.

Import Duties and Customs Fees

Again, this is an area where you need to engage a professional service provider in the territory you are expanding to. A customs broker will handle paying all the import taxes and duties, as well as arranging to pay any customs fees that may be placed on your incoming shipment. Let me emphasize here that this is often not worth doing yourself. Working across timezones, in different languages and with complex customs and tax requirements — there are too many moving parts. If just one thing gets handled incorrectly, the whole operation can come apart, and you'll find your shipment being returned to you at exorbitant rates, instead of being processed and going on to Amazon for distribution. Finding the right brokers is critical to your international expansion. We work with customs brokers all over the world, so when you're ready to plan an inventory shipment into a new territory, visit our Resource Page where we have a list of trusted providers to choose from. We'll make sure you've got everything in place to make sure your first shipment goes as smoothly as possible, and can connect you with the provider that will be the best fit for you.

Chapter Eleven: Exporting to International Territories

Expanding into new territories is an exciting, ambitious undertaking for any business. There are huge opportunities associated with entering a new market that has less competition (and customer bases that are eager for new purchasing options). It's critical, though, that you take a realistic approach to this expansion, both in terms of the amount of work that will be required to execute the plan, and the timeline it will take for you to get established.

The timeline will vary significantly, depending on how organized you are, the time of year, and the type of product you are selling. The workload is more predictable, and we'll cover that shortly, but here are some ballpark figures to set your expectations on how long it will take to get set up in international marketplaces once you've got your tax and import numbers registered in each territory:

- Upload product listings
    - One to five days

- Prepare shipment plan in Seller Central
    - One to three days

- Create account / get quotes from freight forwarders and customs broker
    - One to five days

- Obtain an EORI
    - Three days or less

- Prepare physical shipment and get it to freight forwarder
    - One to 10 days
- Freight shipping time for Air transport (plus customs clearing and deliver to Amazon FC)

- One to two weeks

- Freight Shipping time for Sea transport (plus customs clearing and deliver to Amazon FC)
    - Four to six weeks

- Optional: Translate listings into local language (Germany, Italy, Spain etc)
    - Two to three days

- Set up post-purchase Emails and PPC
    - Emails: One week
    - PPC: Two weeks for keyword research and observing automatic campaigns. Set up and maintain new campaigns, add new campaigns over time based on performance, local holidays, and your own promotional calendar.

All told, the process can take two to four months (and potentially longer if you start moving in Q3 or Q4, going into holiday season). It depends on your warehouse and their capacity for arranging shipments, how long it takes your shipment to arrive (which can be affected by weather, freight schedules and customs delays), and the receiving process at Amazon's end.

Getting Your Inventory Into Europe

The general import duty rate throughout European territories falls between 3-5%. You'll pay this in combination with the VAT for the specified number of units in your shipment at the time the inventory is received at the import location.

All import taxes and customs fees must be paid before your inventory reaches Amazon — if it arrives still owing any money, Amazon will not pay the bill for you. They will reject the shipment and it will be sent all the way back to where you sent it from at an extremely steep rate. It's for this reason that it is critical you have the resources to project-manage a team of vendors — shipping carriers, freight forwarders, and customs brokers — who will handle the importation process, dispatch the customs brokerage, and actually get your inventory to Amazon. Engaging the services of a company who specializes in this process will save you significant amounts of time, stress and money.

There are some air freight providers which bundle freight forwarding *and* customs brokerage into their transport costs, such as DHL and FedEx. Where it makes sense, we do recommend working with end-to-end providers like these so that you only have one point of contact to deal with. However, don't assume that just because you have someone on the ground, you won't have to be involved anymore. Outsourcing a project like this does not mean that the process is guaranteed or that your service provider is going to make all the decisions for you. There are still a lot of decisions for you to make, from approving shipping quotes, coordinating delivery schedules, and overseeing project milestones.

You need to have a significant pool of resources at your disposal to be able to execute an expansion plan effectively. Liquid cash is part of that, of course, but you also need quite a lot of time and energy dedicated to the process in order to make it all happen. For some businesses, that means making it the responsibility of a new or existing team member who can handle all these moving parts. For others (particularly if you have a small team or all your team members are already wearing a lot of hats), it makes more sense to use an agency that has been through the process dozens of times before and can give you guidance on choosing vendors and how the process should unfold.

Hiring A Broker and Freight Forwarder

To find the right customs broker for your business and inventory, you first need to have a shipping plan. A shipping plan is created in Amazon's Seller or Vendor interface and includes the quantity of SKUs being shipped in, and the dimensions and weights of the boxes or cartons that the SKUs are in. Creating an accurate shipping plan is critical to having Amazon receive your inventory expediently. We recommend contacting freight forwarders and customs brokers as you're developing your shipping plan, so that you know what specific information they would require you to provide in order for them to give you an accurate quote when you're ready. The freight forwarder will have a freight quote request form that will detail the next steps in the process for you to work through.

Once you've reached an agreement with a freight forwarder, they will advise you on next steps to actually execute your shipping plan, such as how the inventory should be palletized for each country. They'll arrange the inventory to be shipped from your point of origin, and then will arrange to unload and forward your freight at the point of import at the other end. We can connect you with a selection of freight forwarders and customs brokers that we've worked with and seen a good standard of service from. See the Resources Page (http://www.bobsledmarketing.com/amazon-expansion-plan-resources) on our website.

Your customs broker will process the inventory through customs, pay all the fees and taxes, process all the associated paperwork, and then will oversee the inventory being put on a truck that has scheduled in a delivery time with the relevant Amazon warehouse. It's worth noting that customs brokers and forwarders provide varying levels of service — some providers, like Shapiro, provide both services and can handle sea, air and overland freight in-house. Others will only handle specific aspects of the process.

Getting an EORI and Business Registration Number

The EORI is the Economic Operator Registration and Identification number. This number is assigned by the customs authority in the territory you are dealing with, to be used in all your communications with customs authorities (whether it's you specifically, or your freight forwarder and customs broker). It marks your business as registered and approved to import inventory into the territory, and provides a central identification for all your dealings with the bureaucracy surrounding imports and customs. Your EORI covers you for all European territories, and the Business Registration Number does the same thing for dealing with Canada.

Again, we cover country-specific selling and importation processes and tips in our dedicated Country Guides, which you can find in a special section reserved for readers of this book on the Bobsled Marketing website. Navigate to the Resources Page on our website (http://www.bobsledmarketing.com/amazon-expansion-plan-resources).

Getting Your Inventory Processed Into Amazon's Warehouses

Once your shipment leaves to be sent to another territory, it's really out of your hands until it's in Amazon's warehouses. If something goes wrong, your freight forwarder or customs broker will be the one who handles it — which is why it's so important to work with companies that are experienced and trustworthy. Specifically, they need to have experience with Amazon's process, because they will be the ones to schedule the delivery appointment with Amazon's warehouse, and will be the ones to handle the actual delivery process (which is quite a specific undertaking). They will handle all the processing paperwork when it arrives, and will act as your representative in dealings with third parties.

The reason it's so important that your freight forwarder is familiar with Amazon's processes is that it can throw your timelines off by weeks if they get it wrong. It's the same as the process in the US: A delivery needs to be scheduled — often weeks in advance — and executed very precisely. If the delivery is more than 30 minutes late for the scheduled time, Amazon will not accept the inventory and the freight forwarder will have to reschedule for another delivery slot. It can be between one and three weeks before another time is available (potentially even longer during holiday seasons), so it's key to get this right first time around.

Chapter Twelve: Maximizing Your Amazon Opportunities

Generally speaking, the customers you acquire through Amazon are considered Amazon's customers. You don't get the ability to remarket to them, add them to an email list or newsletter, or even communicate with them directly if you're on the Vendor program. You're limited in what you can do to maximize the lifetime value of that customer, except to use Amazon's messaging system to follow up with them after they've made their purchase (and if you do this, make sure you're not directing them away from Amazon to any other site — this is another thing that can cause an instant ban on your account).

To increase revenue per purchase, you can set up promotions on Amazon where you can offer a 'buy one, get one free' or 'buy one, get the second for less' and so on. These are very easy to set up in the promotions tab in Seller Central.

Now, you can't get customer email addresses from Amazon, but you *can* get their phone numbers. The purpose of this is explicitly for customer support — *do no*t use it to call or text them for marketing purposes — but you can now create a lookalike audience on Facebook's advertising platform from phone numbers. This means you could potentially retarget those customers on Facebook and other advertising platforms. To stay up to date on this strategy, visit the Resource Page for this book and subscribe to our newsletter to stay up to date on how this strategy plays out — there are tools and software in development which can help to automate this process.

You can also choose to limit the products you list on Amazon to a smaller selection of your total product assortment. Many of the brands we talk to at Bobsled Marketing are concerned about the cannibalization issue, and the easiest way to avoid this is to limit Amazon's access to your product line. Instead of listing all, say, 100 of your products on Amazon, you can just list 25. For the remaining 75 products, you get to keep your margins, remarket to your customers, and deal with those customers in whatever way best suits your business.

Another idea is to offer limited edition or special edition products on your ecommerce store to differentiate your own platform from Amazon's. This can be a good way to make sure that Amazon doesn't cannibalize all of your sales. If you promote the additional products or special offers on your social media channels, then the customers who see your insert collateral and follow you might also find a reason to consider making the jump to buying directly from you.

When it comes to maximizing the lifetime value of the customers you acquire through Amazon, you need to take a long view, and avoid trying to 'get around' the limitations they impose on sellers. You're playing in their sandpit, and breaking the rules will get you sent home with nothing to show for it. It's better to work within the system, acknowledge that some customers simply would not have purchased your products at all if they weren't on Amazon. Focus on generating a consistent stream of revenue, rather than trying to eke out just a little bit more and risking getting shut out completely.

Amazon Growth Opportunities

As you become a more substantial seller on Amazon, there may be certain additional privileges extended to you. For example, we worked with a billion-dollar brand which sells via Seller Central. While Seller Central is typically self-service only, because they are such a big brand it's in Amazon's interest to create a strategic partnership with them. Our client received all kinds of perks not usually seen on Seller Central: They have a representative available to talk with about issues related to their account, change details in the system for them, remove unauthorized sellers for them, and other VIP treatment. At this level, Amazon might even code changes directly into Amazon's platform just for them. When you become a big enough player, you gradually get more and more negotiating power with Amazon.

Seller Fulfilled Prime

If you have your own fulfillment capability, this program allows you to ship orders directly to customers as part of the overall Prime program. You have to provide all the same benefits of Prime to customers (free 2-day shipping and free returns being the core ones), but you don't have to send your products to Amazon's fulfillment centers first for them to ship them out. This can potentially end up being more cost effective, as long as you have good rates with your shipping carriers. Customizable shipping templates mean that you can choose which locations you offer Seller Fulfilled Prime in. For example, if your warehouse is located in New Jersey, you may wish to only offer the 2-Day Prime shipping option to customers in the Northeast, ensuring that you can meet Amazon's delivery requirements profitably. This program can be a very good move for larger sellers with established logistics.
However, Amazon fiercely guards the trust that consumers have in the Prime program. So you'll be required to meet some pretty strict performance guidelines to become (and stay) eligible for the program.

We have a detailed White Paper on Seller Fulfilled Prime which outlines the requirements and our recommendations on how brands proceed with the program. It's not for everyone! As a reader of this book you get immediate access to the White Paper by visiting the Resources Page on our website (http://www.bobsledmarketing.com/amazon-expansion-plan-resources).

Amazon For Business

The B2B or business-to-business ecommerce market is *much* bigger than the consumer ecommerce market (in terms of spend). Governments, hospitals, small businesses, manufacturers — they all buy lots of goods, but it's not as 'sexy' as the consumer side. It's harder to do, but Amazon saw a major opportunity here and launched Amazon For

Business in 2015 with an eye on capturing some of the $800 billion B2B ecommerce category.

It's a good move for established retail businesses to start thinking about how their products could be used in a business context. Even if you've never thought of your product as having B2B potential, see if you can come up with an angle that would work. For example, we work with a boutique food retailer, and I've personally purchased their gift baskets as thank-you presents for clients. We've also seen large orders come through around the holiday season, when companies are sending out their annual well-wishes. It's not a business that would traditionally go after the B2B space, but the orders are typically much larger than what they see from the consumer side, so it's been very worthwhile developing this new arm of the business.

Amazon For Business is a closed-access program for buyers and sellers — buyers must provide their EIN and are manually vetted to confirm that they are a business entity. And manufacturers or distributors must apply to sell on the platform. Ultimately, the program lets you sell to pre-vetted procurement buyers and organizations, rather than individuals. Once sellers are admitted to the program, they can take advantage of these program benefits:

- Offer business-only price discounts and quantity pricing. List products and prices specifically for business customers. Create discounts for business customers, and discounts on purchases of larger quantities.

- Display your quality and diversity credentials. List your current credentials to increase purchases from procurement specialists who need to meet quality sourcing objectives and corporate social responsibility goals.

- Add enhanced product content. This can be a substantial benefit for technical products, since you can include useful product information including CAD drawings, user manuals, spec sheets, comparison charts, and installation manuals.

- Create a seller profile page. You can add banners, logos, and information about your company on this page which is not available to regular sellers on Seller Central.

- Enable tax-exempt pricing. Automate tax exemption on qualified purchases from sellers participating in the Amazon Tax-Exemption program.

Given that the program comes at no additional cost to existing sellers, this seems like a no- brainer way to extend your customer base and pay less in Amazon fees. If you don't have a wholesale line sheet or capability to track and fill Purchase Orders from business customers, this can be a great way to work with organizations who wish to buy products in bulk from your company. We have a White Paper with more detail on this program on our Resources page, dedicated to readers of this book, at http://www.bobsledmarketing.com/amazon-expansion-plan-resources

Chapter Thirteen: What To Do Next

So you've been through this book, and now you have a few decisions to make. First and foremost, are you going to start implementing all these processes yourself, or hire a consultant or agency to help you?

Your company could certainly manage all these processes internally. The information is out there and it's not that hard to find — it *is* possible to accomplish everything we've talked about on your own or with a small team. The challenge is implementation, and this is where people get stuck.

You might have an intuitive understanding of how and why all these processes work and fit together, but there's a big difference between that and actually building the solution into your business and implementing it day in and day out. You need to have a very clear picture of who will be responsible for what, and how adding this channel into the mix is going to change the daily function of your business.

Alternately, if you're going to work with an Amazon agency, which one is the right fit for your business? The checklist below will help you find the right fit to help you grow your Amazon presence.

How to Make Sure Your Amazon Agency Is Up to Scratch

If you do decide to choose an agency, it's critical that you find one that knows what they're doing and has a deep understanding of everything we've covered in this book. Managing your Amazon presence is a critical undertaking that has real consequences for your business, so I suggest using the following checklist when making your decision about working with any agency:

- **Do they have verifiable, direct experience?**

    - Any agency worth their salt will have happy customers who are willing to share their success stories. If there are no testimonials or case studies, there are two explanations: either the agency is completely new (which can translate to a lot of 'trial and error' activity) or they haven't been able to get any results (which, obviously, you don't want to deal with). They should have a great reputation that precedes them and demonstrated expertise you can rely on. In the later stages of selecting a consultant or agency, it is entirely acceptable to ask to speak directly with current or past clients to verify the inevitably glowing case studies and testimonials.

- **Do they have all the necessary experts on their team to make every part of your Amazon strategy a success?**
    - *The Project Manager:* this person is accountable for results in this sales channel. They may be testing the effectiveness of some new campaign or tactic, but the overall revenue results are their main KPI. They also keep everyone on the team on schedule and on budget. This individual must have deep experience on the relevant Amazon selling platform - Vendor Central, Seller Central, or both - in order to see around corners and anticipate the impacts of new programs or changes to terms of service which seem to spring up every week or so within Amazon's landscape.
    - *The PPC Manager:* this is a very specific area of expertise, and you won't get good results from advertising if this happens in tandem with a long list of other responsibilities. This person must have a head for keyword research, tracking performance reports, and endlessly tweaking and creating campaigns to refine results. Keeping up to date with the constant changes to the Amazon PPC algorithm, and reviewing and tweaking campaigns at least twice-weekly should be part of their job description. This individual must have direct experience with Amazon's PPC systems - Amazon Marketing Services (AMS) and/or Sponsored Products. Asking a PPC generalist who knows their way around the Facebook or Google advertising platforms is not enough. Your Amazon PPC Specialist must

grok all the upstream effects on PPC campaigns (Buy Box ownership, retail pricing, product reviews, product titles) as well as deeply understanding your brand and its product assortment.

- *The Creatives:* talented copywriters and designers are often brought in on a project or freelance basis, and their value in helping sales conversion cannot be understated. Effectively communicating the features and benefits of a product, while staying 'on-brand' is a critical piece of on-page optimization.
- *Customer Service:* unless your brand is on the Vendor Central or Vendor Express platform, there will be some customer service involved with running your Amazon channel. Customers ask questions about product functionality, how to return or exchange merchant-fulfilled items, and all sorts of random queries. This person needs to be responsible for responding to all customer inquiries within a 24-hour period. They need to check the account daily to respond to messages and reviews, review account performance metrics, chase up unauthorized sellers and to flag any other issues with operations or PPC.

In theory, these roles could be handled by a couple of people, but they're very distinct roles and a reputable agency will have different people handling each role. Whatever agency you choose, make sure there is someone who is specifically accountable for each of these activities on Amazon.

- **Will the agency get on the phone with you?**
  - Most agencies will have a screening process to make sure that both parties would be a good fit (at least on paper) to work together. The screening will usually be a simple survey or questionnaire to ensure that you have the type of business they specialize in helping. Not every client is the right for for every agency, so this is an important filter for both parties.

    - Pay attention to how responsive the individual or agency is in the sales process. If it takes days for them to get back to your initial or follow-up inquiry, it could be a sign that they are overwhelmed with other client work and don't have the resources to give your account the attention that it needs.

- **Do they have a well-defined process?**
    - Can they communicate exactly how they deliver on what they're promising? What is their step-by-step process from the day they start work on your account, through to the point that everything is in place and has shifted into maintenance mode? Does this line up with the processes we've outlined in this book?
    - If you're launching a new account or new product, you should expect that they have a launch-specific process. They should be able to articulate exactly how they're going to go through the launch process, as distinct from their general account management processes, which needs to be defined by the daily, weekly, and monthly tasks they implement for each account. The launch process is also different to managing and optimizing a 'mature' account, as is managing only the paid advertising on an Amazon account. Understand what activities the consultant or agency will be doing on a monthly basis and how it will be reported.

- **How do they charge?**
    - Some agencies will work on a performance basis, while others charge flat fees, or monthly retainers, and others still will have a blend of those options. Some will have different arrangements depending on the type of business in question, but regardless of what they tell you, make sure that there's a very clear understanding of what you'll be charged for the engagement.
    - As a general rule, established agencies like Bobsled Marketing who have a lot of demand from new clients generally don't take on performance-

based work for clients. If performance-based fees is the only model that your company will accept, you may be limited to less experienced consultants or agencies who are in the early stages of proving their process.

    - Consider how your Amazon sales channel is affected by other marketing channels. If you're running a PR or social advertising campaign that picks up steam, your Amazon sales will get a natural lift from this. This means your performance-based fees will start adding up. And from the agency's standpoint, they are taking a risk around payments given that they are not in control of inventory. They could be doing the best work possible on your account, only to have sales stall if your company runs into supply chain issues that they agency has no control over.
    - Some advertising-focused agencies will charge a percentage of Ad spend, while others will only accept a monthly retainer. Be sure you understand the agency's process here, because an agency that is incentivized to spend more budget on PPC may be less careful about making those campaigns efficient and profitable for you.

- **What other channels or marketplaces does the agency support?**
    - If it's an Amazon-only agency, then you can expect them to have a very deep understanding and insight into Amazon's processes. If it's important to you to work with an agency that also handles other marketplaces, then it's key that they're able to give you clear, precise information about each one.

Could Bobsled Marketing Be The Right Agency For You?

We offer a full, done-for-you Amazon service. We do launch strategy and implementation, optimize your existing Amazon sales channel to grow it to the next level, as well as handle all the administrative and operational sides of managing an account (responding to customer enquiries, feedback and reviews, checking your inventory levels, helping you with assortment planning and so on), auditing and improving your PPC strategy and campaigns, and all the other day-to-day aspects of running your Amazon sales channel.

With an Amazon-focused agency handling the logistics, you get to skip the learning curve, and the common mistakes that can stall your growth on Amazon. In researching this book, I tallied the number of individual processes and procedures that we use at Bobsled Marketing to help our clients launch, optimize, and troubleshoot issues on their Amazon account. We have over 100 processes, templates, and checklists which are used every week by our team to keep all accounts running smoothly.

Many of those processes are done just once during an Amazon product launch, or if something goes wrong like an unauthorized seller is selling a counterfeit version of your product. By managing accounts and troubleshooting all day, every day, we are able to identify and quickly take advantage of new opportunities and nip problems in the bud. This would take inexperienced sellers days or weeks to figure out alone.

Then there are the 10 things we do every day, week and month for every account we manage. These are just the things that keep the lights on — the basics that have to be handled to make sure the store keeps functioning — because most of our clients don't want to add extra people to their teams to handle all of this in-house. This includes monitoring and taking action against unauthorized sellers, monitoring inventory levels and generating demand forecasts, checking and responding to customer questions, feedback, and product reviews, reconciling inbound inventory shipments, and more.

We use a swag of software, some proprietary, which helps streamline some of the processes around account reporting, PPC campaign monitoring, automating customer messages and responses, and identifying areas of an account to dive deeper on. But even the best software in the world isn't helpful if you don't know how to interpret the output and make smart decisions on it. This is where human-powered insight is required.

Our other services include PPC account management for both Sponsored Products (Seller Central) and Amazon Marketing Services (Vendor Central), and the Amazon Advertising Platform. We help people to optimize their Vendor or Seller Central accounts, as well as special projects, including custom consultations and account audits.

***

Having an Amazon expert manage your account also frees up your time to focus on finding more growth opportunities for your business. Most companies view Amazon as one of several sales channels for their brand. As anyone who has tried to spin a lot of plates knows, it's difficult to manage and grow many different sales, distribution, and marketing channels all at once.

Effective, sustainable product companies never rest on their laurels when it comes to product development. There are always improvements to make, features to implement, new versions to launch, new seasons and trends to consider, new ways to drive down costs and increase profits.

Product and business development activities are strategic, effective ways to drive down costs, reach more consumers, and increase profits. Business Owners, Marketers, Brand Managers, and Leaders of Sales & Business Development need to allocate their time and resources wisely. Freeing up your company's time to spend on strategic business and product development will give you better leverage than wrestling with product feeds, nerding out on the latest Amazon strategy, or monitoring for unauthorized sellers.

Amazon is constantly evolving their terms of service, search and PPC algorithms, platform capabilities, and launching new programs such as an exclusive 'Professional Beauty' designation in the beauty category, Fashion Accelerator for wholesale suppliers to Amazon's private label brands, and 'Transparency' barcoding to curb counterfeit goods. All this change can be hard to keep up with. But when you work with a laser focused Amazon agency, you have an A-list team keeping up with all these developments and identifying how these changes could possibly help or hinder your business. We discuss all these evolutions at length in our email newsletter, which you can sign up for at www.bobsledmarketing.com/subscribe.

Whether it's launching the Amazon For Business or Seller Fulfilled Prime Programs, changes to the way product listings are displayed or new brand legitimacy requirements, it's all up for real-time discussion in our newsletter, so I'd love to have you join us. Keeping up with Amazon is a job in and of itself, so let us help you keep ahead of it all. This way, when Amazon launches a new feature or changes their terms of service, you get actionable analysis on what it really means and how it's going to impact your business.

And if you're considering getting help starting on Amazon, or optimizing your business, Bobsled Marketing might just be the solution you're looking for. Our Amazon Project Managers and PPC Managers handle the Amazon marketplace channel for clients that range from crowdfunded hardware startups to billion-dollar consumer brands. We can help with:

- Planning and implementing your brand's launch on Amazon in the US or international marketplaces

- Expert management and optimization of your Amazon PPC campaigns

- Consultations, account audits and implementation support for existing Sellers who need expert help identifying how to grow revenue on Amazon.

Connect with us in the way that suits you best: We have the Facebook Group, our weekly email newsletter (you can sign up for that at www.bobsledmarketing.com/subscribe). If you'd rather reach out to me directly, email kmasters@bobsledmarketing.com.

How long before I start seeing results?

How long will it take for my brand to start seeing results on Amazon? This is a question we often get from prospective clients. But the real question that's being asked is how long will *Bobsled Marketing* take to deliver results?

While we can't see into the future and predict exactly what is going to happen with each brand we work with, we can use data and experience to give you a good idea.

The majority of brands Bobsled works with will see results, in the form of Amazon sales, within the first 2-3 months of working with us. Some elements (like PPC advertising) will start seeing results sooner, and some harder to reach goals (like a healthy flow of buyer reviews) will take a little longer.

The time it takes to reach your sales goals is partially dependent upon the category your product falls into, as well as how much of the strategy is already in motion.

Brands we partner with to launch on Amazon for the first time typically start seeing significant results on Amazon within the first 3 months after launch, with several of our brands reaching halfway to their targeted average monthly sales volumes by that point.

And by the 6-month mark, many brands can expect to see their sales volume double what it was at the 3-month mark.

Brands that are already established on Amazon may ask what Bobsled can do that you're not already doing in your account. The answer here is that we bring our extensive Amazon expertise to the table, with a team comprised of ex-Amazonians, experienced project managers, and PPC experts. After partnering with Bobsled, our clients see on average over 100% increase in average monthly sales by months 4-6.

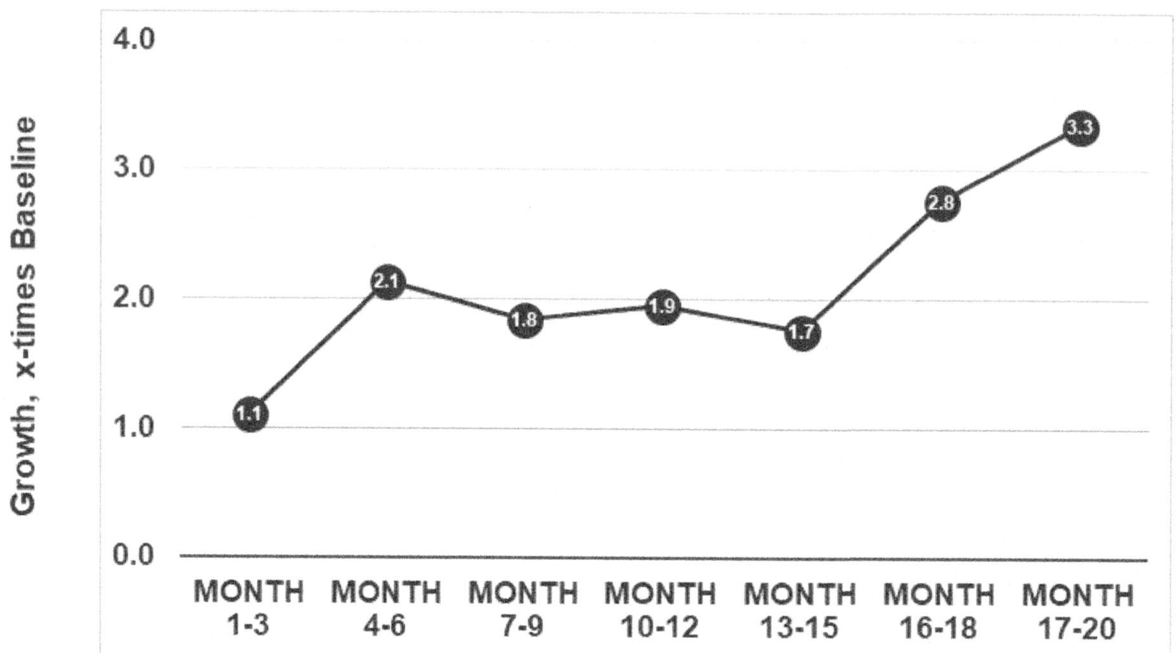

Average Monthly Sales Growth Multiple from Baseline*

*Baseline is average monthly sales in the three months before partnering with Bobsled

This 100% growth rate is based on the results from 13 account management clients we're working with at the time of writing. We took their average product sales during the three months prior to Bobsled partnership ("baseline"), and then calculated the average sales growth we saw from the subsequent three month periods relative to that original baseline value.

From our analysis we show that Bobsled sees over 10% increase in our brand's average monthly sales in the first three months and over 110% increase in sales in the four to six month period. This growth continues throughout the first year of our partnership as we refine our strategies and we learn what works best for you and your brand. By the year and a half mark, we typically see further leaps in growth as our brands succeed in the marketplace and we partner with the brand to launch new products, and sometimes new marketplaces. And finally, to cap off all the directional and theoretical information packed into this book, I'd like to share some real stories of how Bobsled Marketing has helped our clients to launch and grow on Amazon.

Case Study 1: Brand Launch on Amazon Seller Central

Our client is positioned well in the sporting goods category, which is a highly competitive category, but has also seen sales growth of 11% year-over-year on Amazon (source: One Click Retail, January 2018).

They had previously been invited to sell on Amazon as Vendors, but opted to proceed on the Seller Central Marketplace for more control over their product assortment, pricing, and availability. The client wanted to launch in various international marketplaces, and recognized the need for expert support to outline the strategy and process, and also implement the launched.

How Bobsled Marketing helped

This brand took advantage of Bobsled's industry expertise to launch their brand on Amazon with A+ content, optimized product pages, professional images, a comprehensive promotion strategy, and inventory forecasts to make sure their product inventory was meeting demand.

Because of this success, the brand confidently expanded to Canada in month 7 and the United Kingdom and Germany in month 8. Now this brand is bringing in an average of $63k in monthly sales that didn't exist before they launched on Amazon.

The Results

- The brand went from $0 in monthly sales to $63,000 in monthly sales in an 8 month period.
- By month 2 the brand had reached half its current average sales volume and continued to climb for the following six months to the month 8 average of $63,000.
- The brand continues to see excellent PPC performance with ACoS (Advertising Cost of Sales) typically less than 2.0%.

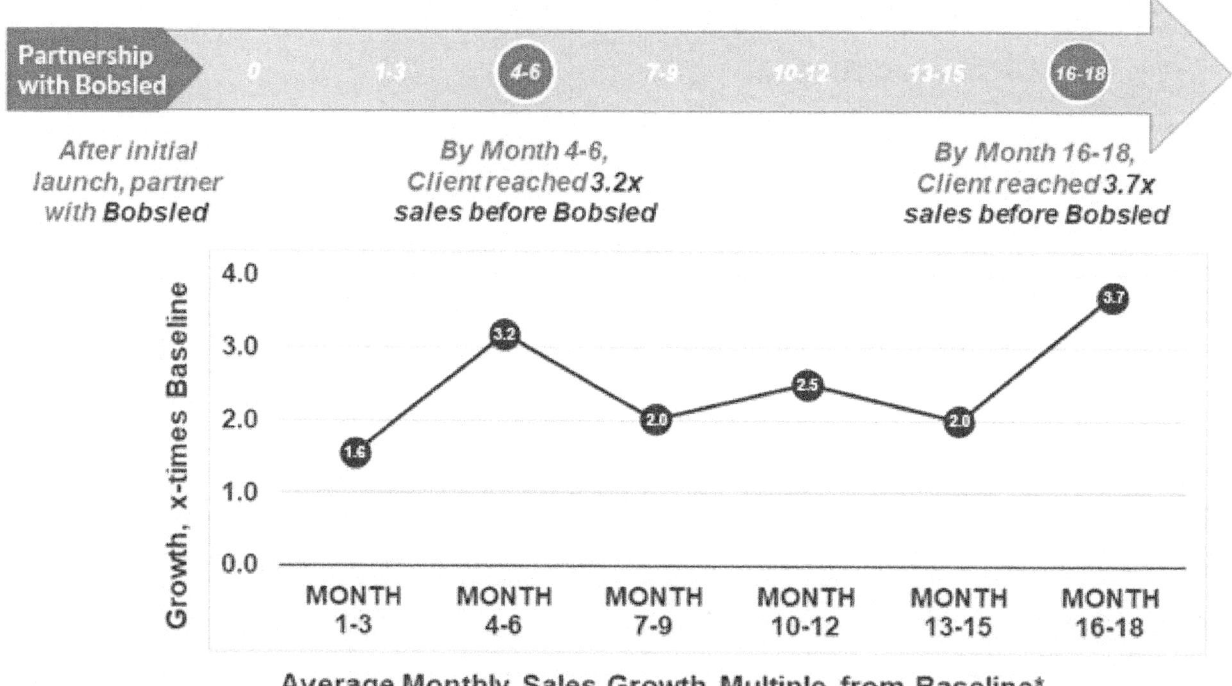

*Baseline is average monthly sales in the three months before partnering with Bobsled

Case Study 2: Optimizing an existing Amazon Vendor Central account

The client is a branded manufacturer of a popular wireless hearing and listening system, specifically marketed toward people with hearing loss. They were already established as a Vendor on Amazon, but felt like they weren't maximizing the opportunity on the channel. They approached Bobsled to help grow sales and manage their channel to free up time and attention to focus on their core retail channel.

While there were individuals within the company who were accountable for results on Amazon, there was a lack of expertise around how to manage the channel. Part of this included challenges with communicating with Amazon. Although the brand had been assigned a Vendor Manager at Amazon, these individuals are tasked with managing dozens of brand accounts, and simply didn't' have a lot of time to spend with each account.

Other issues:

- Struggling to grow their sales on Amazon—the client didn't have the time necessary to dedicate to optimizing campaigns and understanding the marketplace.
- A previous Craigslist hire lead to heavy ad spending with little results.
- The popularity of their product lead to several unauthorized sellers competing for the Buy Box on their product pages.
- Responding to negative reviews in a timely manner was difficult.
- Amazon was pricing a core product above MSRP, causing depressed sales for this product. Despite ongoing requests from both the client and Bobsled, Amazon would not lower it to an acceptable price.

How Bobsled Marketing helped

Before officially signing on with Bobsled for an ongoing management retainer, we began with a comprehensive client account audit. This audit included a review of listing pages, analysis of current PPC efforts, and in-depth keyword research.

While completing this audit we identified a laundry list of changes to make to differentiate their product listings over the competition, including reviewing each product listing to address both desktop and mobile shoppers.

We also addressed key issues with their existing Amazon Marketing Services (AMS) campaigns and grow sales for the brand while keeping ACoS low.

Since signing on Bobsled for comprehensive management of their account, the team assigned to this client began to systematically remove unauthorized sellers. At the same time, we developed an ongoing process for dealing with negative product reviews and posting responses on the client's behalf.

The results

- In the one to three month period immediately following our partnership we saw average monthly sales increase by a factor of 1.6x baseline (or a 60% increase in sales). In the next three months we saw sales increase by a factor of 3.2x baseline (or a 220% increase in sales).
- Significantly fewer unauthorized sellers on the client's listing pages.
- A single Sponsored Products campaign has generated more than $660,000 since March 2016, with an ACoS of 3.88%.
- From Q4 2016 to Q1 2017, we more than doubled the number of product reviews on this account, with some products increasing by 270% to 450%. Most importantly, the star ratings stabilized across the board, from having several products with 3.5 star ratings, to all products now having 4+ stars.

Bobsled Marketing Testimonials

"I have been really pleased with the Bobsled Marketing team. I knew the project would be a special challenge, but I only have great things to say about the Bobsled Marketing team."

— Anne Coelen, Director of Marketing, eCommerce at Playboy Enterprises

"We have been impressed by Bobsled Marketing's weekly contact and checklists throughout the process, and look forward to growing this business together."
— Jim Dygas, Owner of Urban Accents

"I chose to work with Bobsled to grow my brand on Amazon because I needed help with the many aspects of marketing, inventory management, customer feedback, listing optimizations, etc.

My company was assigned to work with Lori Dinkins, who we have worked with now for the past 3 months. From day 1, I have felt like Lori is an actual stakeholder in the business. She actually cares about it as much as I do! She has a very broad understanding of Amazon and what it takes to move the needle. More importantly, Lori has helped my brand in ways that I didn't even know it needed. We have sync up calls every couple of weeks for her to report progress, but she is available anytime we need her.

I have zero reservations in recommending bobsled to anyone wanting to hire a superstar on their team."

— Ryan Dewey, Co-Founder, Hollystone Inc

"We were just looking at the company bank account and loving all those bombs you're dropping! We are so grateful for your excellent work, you have excelled in every aspect of your job."
— Shannon Drake, Founder of Give Me The Dirt

"We have been Amazon direct vendors for nearly 10 years now and have seen the platform change (visibility, AMS, etc.), requiring additional management. Our Bobsled

Marketing team is constantly in touch and involved in all pending issues. Our AMS campaigns have increased efficiency with the management from our team, as well as resulted in increased sales.

As being a proactive, involved and informed Amazon vendor for many years, the Bobsled team has complemented our mindset perfectly."
— Bobsled Marketing Client, Published on Web Retailer

"We had been putting off the idea of launching our products on Amazon because of the competition in our categories. From my first call with Tom and Kiri I could tell that they had the experience and skills to help us launch our products effectively."
— Tyler Condie, Founder of Rugged Material

Want to explore working with us to bring the same results into your business?
Head to http://www.bobsledmarketing.com/contact/,
fill out the questionnaire, and we'll be in touch.

Thank you for taking the time to read *The Amazon Expansion Plan.* I hope it proves to be a powerful resource for your brand's growth on Amazon.

I love sharing my knowledge about ecommerce and selling on Amazon - and the things we do every day for clients at Bobsled Marketing.

I would be honored to get your thoughts on this book and news of how it helped you optimize and grow your company's Amazon sales channel.

Now that you know how important reviews are on Amazon, I hope you can take a minute to write a genuine review of the book on Amazon.

KIRI MASTERS

Kiri is the founder and CEO of Bobsled Marketing, an Amazon marketing agency, and the Author of "The Amazon Expansion Plan".

She holds a Bachelor of Marketing & Public Relations from the University of Notre Dame Australia. She is a contributor to Forbes.com, where she writes about how Amazon and similar marketplaces affect consumer brands.

Kiri is on the RetailWire panel of retail experts, the winner of a Silver Stevie® Award for Young Female Entrepreneur of the Year, and one of the co-hosts of the Ecommerce Braintrust podcast.

Made in the USA
Monee, IL
27 January 2021